THEMES
OF
THE

ON
Macroeconomics

**A COLLECTION
OF ARTICLES FROM**

The New York Times

Boston San Francisco New York
London Toronto Sydney Tokyo Singapore Madrid
Mexico City Munich Paris Cape Town Hong Kong Montreal

Senior Acquisitions Editor:	Adrienne D'Ambrosio
Editorial Assistant:	Meg Beste
Senior Marketing Manager:	Roxanne Hoch
Managing Editor:	Nancy Fenton
Manufacturing Buyer:	Carol Melville
Composition:	Argosy Publishing

Cover Image: © Mike Bentley from www.istockphoto.com/abzee

ISBN 0-321-49292-7

All articles included in *Themes of the Times on Macroeconomics* are copyrighted by The New York Times Company and reprinted with permission.

Many of the designations used by manufacturers and sellers to distinguish their products are claimed as trademarks. Where those designations appear in this book, and Addison-Wesley was aware of a trademark claim, the designations have been printed in initial caps or all caps.

3 4 5 6 7 8 9 10—CRS—10 09 08 07

Macroeconomics

Contents

Public Health Measures Always Involve Trade-Offs

By ALAN B. KRUEGER—March 31, 2005

IN extraordinary circumstances like this," President Bush said of the Terri Schiavo predicament, "it is wisest to always err on the side of life."

Uwe E. Reinhardt, a Princeton University health economist, said that from his perspective President Bush was not quite right: the president should have said "err on the side of life years."

There are two reasons for this distinction. First, no action can save a life indefinitely; life can only be extended. Saving the life of an infant leads to more expected life years than saving the life of a centenarian.

Second, health economists are typically concerned with finding policies that maximize the total number of life years, or, equivalently, the average life expectancy of the population, leaving aside quality-of-life issues for now. A focus on life years recognizes that there are inevitable trade-offs involved in health and safety policies.

One can believe that life is sacred and still recognize that trade-offs exist. If government policy always erred on the side of life, the speed limit would be reduced to 5 miles per hour to eliminate all fatal accidents. Of course, voters would not stand for a 5 m.p.h. speed limit, so at least implicitly policy makers recognize that there is a trade-off between risk and the time required to transport goods and people on the highways.

This principle was clearly stated by the Office of Management and Budget in the 2003 budget: "Since the nation does not possess enough resources to eliminate all risks, an important performance goal for government is to deploy risk-management resources in a way that achieves the greatest public health improvement for the resources available."

Yet research indicates that the government generally does a poor job in choosing policies that maximize life years. Many programs are intended to reduce the risk of premature death. If the government used its limited budget to maximize the number of life years, the cost of saving an additional life year would be the same across different programs.

In actuality, the cost per year of life saved varies widely across regulations and programs. Some cost-effective initiatives that would reduce risks are passed over, while others that are more costly and less effective are put in place.

For example, a program of prenatal care for pregnant women is estimated to cost $2,800 per year of life saved, while the cost per year of life saved from regulating airborne benzene is around $5 million.

A 1995 study by public health specialists of 587 possible life-saving interventions found that a quarter of them cost less than $6,900 per year of life saved and a quarter cost more than $372,000 per year of life saved (updated to 2005 dollars)—a ratio of more than 50 to 1. In general, safety standards and preventive medical treatments were more cost-effective than environmental regulations.

Why does the cost per life year saved differ so much across policies?

There are two main explanations. First, the government may get things wrong. There is no mechanism to make the government pursue the most cost-effective strategies because agency budgets are monitored by different Congressional committees and because the costs of complying with regulations are not counted in the federal budget. As a result, regulations may appear to be less expensive than programs that are more cost-effective but require direct government spending.

Lobbying by vested interests may also lead policy makers to stray from the most efficient risk reduction programs.

Second, the public may value some programs more than others for reasons other than the programs' ability to save lives, and policy makers may be carrying out the voters' wishes. For example, people may prefer that the government reduce lung cancer by regulating pollution instead of by providing antismoking education, even if the number of life years saved and costs are identical. Such preferences may arise because people let their emotions get in the way of reason. Or the public may view reducing risks differently if the exposure to the risk is voluntary (smoking) as opposed to involuntary (pollution).

To learn how the public evaluates programs intended to reduce premature deaths, Uma Subramanian of the World Bank and Maureen Cropper of the University of Maryland presented 1,013 people with hypothetical choices between pairs of lifesaving programs, like controlling radon in homes versus banning pesticides on fruit. Participants were told to suppose that each program had the same cost and would save the same number of lives each year. After participants selected a program that they thought was best for society, they were asked whether they would switch if the other program saved more lives, with the specific number of extra lives saved randomly assigned in each case.

The researchers found that both the number of lives saved and the characteristics of the programs mattered. When the costs and number of lives saved were the same, a majority of respondents favored cutting pollution over cutting smoking, screening for colon cancer, requiring dual air bags in cars or providing pneumonia vaccinations. Seventy-two percent of the participants favored banning pesticides over controlling radon in homes.

At a given cost and number of lives saved, the participants were more likely to support programs that were geared toward risks that could not easily be controlled, that were more serious, that affected them personally and that were more immediate. Other research by psychologists finds that people prefer to reduce risks that are dreaded and unfamiliar.

Still, participants put tremendous weight on the number of lives saved by a particular program. Of the six pairs of programs considered, a majority never favored a less effective program if the number of lives saved was 2.15 times that in the more effective program.

Bearing in mind that costs were assumed to be equal in the hypothetical comparisons, this range is much smaller than the range in cost per lives saved in actual government programs, suggesting that the public would like policy makers to put more weight on finding the most cost-effective ways to extend lives. Of course, actual decisions are more complicated than hypothetical ones because of issues like quality of life. But a focus on maximizing life years makes the trade-offs clear.

Instead of focusing on one tragic case that most Americans considered a private matter, Congress and the president would have better served the public interest if they had sought to align public policy with voters' interests in maximizing the number of life years saved. Infant mortality, for example, is lower in Cuba than in the United States, according to the 2005 C.I.A. World Factbook. It is hard to believe that a government focused on maximizing life years could not do better.

Alan B. Krueger is the Bendheim professor of economics and public affairs at Princeton University. E-mail: akrueger@ princeton.edu.

The Oil Uproar That Isn't

By JAD MOUAWAD and MATTHEW L. WALD—July 12, 2005

WHEN oil prices spiked in the early 1980's after the Iranian revolution, Jared Nedzel gave up his 1978 Pontiac Trans Am, an emblematic American muscle car, for a smaller, less extravagant Toyota Corolla. He was on his way to Cornell University to study civil engineering and he needed a more economical car.

Today, Mr. Nedzel, a 44-year-old software developer who lives near Boston, owns a Toyota 4Runner, a sport utility vehicle he bought two years ago. It gets about 17.5 miles per gallon, as much as the Trans Am did, and he uses it for his 45-minute commute to work and for driving near the beaches of Martha's Vineyard to get to his favorite fishing spots.

Gasoline prices have spiked again, to more than $2.25 for a gallon of regular in Boston last week, just above the national average, according to the AAA. But energy costs do not weigh on Mr. Nedzel's mind. "Just another gas crisis," he said, expressing an opinion held by many others. "I'm not hyperventilating about it."

For Americans, oil shocks no longer seem so shocking.

The Arab oil embargo of 1973 and the Iranian revolution in 1978–79 exposed America's vulnerability to powerful forces outside its control, forces that sent fuel prices to record levels, prompted anger over gas lines and led to bookend recessions that defined a decade of economic turmoil.

By 1980, the energy crisis and the inflation it spawned had left Americans in a vindictive mood, contributing to the re-election defeat of President Jimmy Carter, who had promised to wage the "moral equivalent of war" against dependence on foreign oil.

But the latest escalation in oil prices—to as much as $60 today from less than $30 a barrel a little more than two years ago—has produced a much more limited response. Energy legislation that President Bush is pressing Congress to pass this summer would bring little relief. And while Americans say in polls that they are deeply disturbed by high gasoline prices and looking for someone to blame, most people continue to drive just as avidly as before; purchases of gas-guzzling sport utility vehicles have slowed but there has been no significant shift to more fuel-efficient cars.

Furthermore, gasoline consumption has continued to rise, up 1 percent in May compared with the same month last year.

James R. Schlesinger, whom President Carter selected as the first energy secretary, in 1977, said in a recent interview that the country's basic energy approach can best be summed up this way: "We have only two modes—complacency and panic."

The earlier oil shocks produced remarkable changes, including the rise of the Japanese auto industry as Americans turned to smaller, more efficient cars out of choice and necessity. With carrots and sticks, the United States managed to cut, temporarily, energy use per person and to scale back the share of oil in its overall energy mix.

The federal government established a strategic petroleum reserve as an insurance policy against global supply disruptions, set a national 55 m.p.h. speed limit and spent billions—much of it wasted, however, on alternatives like shale oil that proved far too costly, particularly after crude oil prices fell when economic recession tempered the demand for energy.

But this time around, the government has done almost nothing to reduce the nation's vulnerability to a sudden interruption in oil supplies. Even the advocates for the long-stalled energy bill that has finally passed both houses of Congress—though in radically different forms—acknowledge that neither version of the measure will be effective.

This month, the House and the Senate will attempt to hammer out their differences and produce the first piece of energy legislation in four years, one that President Bush hopes to sign as early as August.

Crude oil imports have doubled over the last three decades, and now account for nearly two-thirds of the oil Americans burn. Before the 1973 oil embargo, imports accounted for only about one-third of America's energy consumption. In the same three-decade period, oil demand in the United States has grown by 18 percent while domestic production has continued on a slow and probably irrevocable path of decline.

The problem is not the latest price rise, which, adjusted for inflation, is still well below the peak in early 1981, when oil cost the equivalent of $86 a barrel in today's dollars; gasoline, released from price controls, briefly sold back then for the equivalent of $3 a gallon. And it is not just imports; even if the country produced enough oil to meet its domestic needs, in a global economy a price shock would still be felt in the United States.

The fundamental problem, experts say, is that Americans depend almost exclusively on relatively large and heavy private vehicles, virtually all of them running on gasoline, for crucial daily tasks like getting to work and taking their children to school. "Americans live in a car-driven culture where they want to do as much as possible as fast as possible," said Amy Myers Jaffe, the associate director of Rice University's energy program in Houston. "I can drop off my dry cleaning, pick up my prescription drugs, do my banking and buy my lunch, all without leaving my car."

Because of this high dependence on private cars, the United States continues to use oil considerably less efficiently than any other rich industrial country. Yet most of the proposed policy remedies are meant only to subsidize the produc-tion of oil, not use less of it. Many of the rest are focused on electricity, little of it produced by oil.

Despite the lessons of the past, the United States remains particularly vulnerable to a decision by a crucial supplier—for example, the anti-American government of Venezuela—to cut its oil exports, as Saudi Arabia and other Arab nations did in 1973.

Even more critically, Americans can no longer count on abundant supplies of cheap fossil fuels, because developing nations like China and India are emerging as major competitors for resources. This is occurring just as global oil production may be hitting a plateau, a growing number of specialists say. Worldwide output, now about 80 million barrels a day, may fall short of the 100 million barrels a day that energy officials are counting on reaching within the next decade, they say.

Oil prices fell after previous shocks because recessions reduced demand. This time around, galloping consumption has left many authorities believing that the world may face a long period of high prices and tight supplies.

So who is responsible for the current situation? The evidence shows that consumers, oil suppliers, lobbyists and politicians all have played roles.

"A message of the late 1970's is we must prepare for the day of reckoning, the transition away from oil," said Mr. Schlesinger, who also served under President Richard M. Nixon as defense secretary and director of the Central Intelligence Agency.

But it did not happen then, he said, and "I doubt we're going to do it now."

THE CONSUMERS
What Has 4 Wheels and Guzzles Gasoline?

The failure to control consumption is most glaring in the country's transportation sector, which now represents two-thirds of all oil demand in the United States and is solely accountable for the growth of the nation's oil thirst over the last three decades. Each day, America's fleet of more than 200 million cars guzzles 11 percent of the world's daily oil output. Gasoline consumption has risen 35 percent since 1973, compared with a 19 percent increase in overall crude oil consumption.

The growth comes mainly from light trucks, including sport utility vehicles, which account for almost half of all cars sold in the United States. For many consumers, the advantages of an S.U.V.—size, power and an increased sense of security from driving a taller vehicle—largely overshadow one of their main drawbacks, higher fuel consumption.

"Don't blame S.U.V. drivers," said Mr. Nedzel, the 4Runner owner. "The marketplace has changed since the 1970's, and carmakers have adapted and people's habits have changed. For me, there isn't a hybrid that would get me where I want to go."

And while he says he would be willing to tolerate higher gasoline taxes, Mr. Nedzel opposes more stringent fuel efficiency standards. "That's like having an obesity problem," he said, "and being told you need a smaller shirt."

THE INDUSTRY
Supply and Demand Isn't What It Used to Be

On a warm, sunny day in February, David J. O'Reilly, one of

America's top oil executives, stood before 200 energy leaders, analysts and bankers in Houston to lay out what he considered the world's new energy quandary.

"The most visible element of this new equation," said Mr. O'Reilly, the chief executive of Chevron, "is that relative to demand, oil is no longer in plentiful supply. The time when we could count on cheap oil and even cheaper natural gas is clearly ending."

That's a challenge the oil industry is struggling to meet. Major oil companies are fast running out of places to invest for new supplies of oil since most of the world's reserves are in countries that are either wary of foreign investors or, because of war or sanctions, shut off to American oil concerns.

At the same time, the oil industry is waking up to the growing challenge of Asian rivals who are seeking to secure access to their own reserves around the world. Mr. O'Reilly experienced this aggressive new stance first-hand recently: the China National Offshore Oil Corporation is seeking to buy Unocal with an unsolicited $18.5 billion bid and thwart his own offer.

"The main question is access to resources," said Daniel Yergin, chairman of Cambridge Energy Research Associates, an industry consulting firm. "It's the dominant issue that hangs over the entire industry, whether you're talking about Russia, the Middle East, or off the shores of the United States."

In contrast to previous oil shocks, which were caused by unexpected limitations on supply, today's sharp rise in oil prices is almost entirely driven by increased demand, not just from the United States but also from China, India and elsewhere.

According to Mr. O'Reilly, it took 125 years to consume a trillion barrels of oil; the next trillion is likely to be consumed in just 35 years.

To many in the industry, the only realistic alternative is to expand the search for oil, even to areas that are currently closed to drilling, including the ocean off the coasts of California and Florida and the coastal plain of the Arctic National Wildlife Preserve in Alaska.

"We're a spoiled nation," said James T. Hackett, the president and chief executive of the Anadarko Petroleum Corporation and a vocal advocate for increased domestic production. "Because this is such an important national issue, you shouldn't allow yourself to get into a crisis before acting."

But many outside the industry say that intensive exploration of the United States over more than a century has found almost all the oil there is to find, so reversing the decline in domestic production through new discoveries will prove impossible. There is also some doubt about whether oil producers can increase world output enough to keep up with the expected growth in demand.

"Oil supplies will diminish, that's geology," said Kenneth S. Deffeyes, a professor emeritus of geology at Princeton University and the author of "Beyond Oil: The View From Hubbert's Peak" (Hill Wang, 2005). Professor Deffeyes predicts that global oil production will reach its peak around Thanksgiving Day and decline after that. "The negligence comes from doing nothing about alternative fuels or conservation measures over the past 20 years. Now it is too late. The oil is gone."

After previous disruptions, as when the Organization of the Petroleum Exporting Countries took control of their oil resources from foreign oil companies like Chevron in the late 1960's and early 1970's, those companies managed to rebound when high oil prices let them develop high-cost regions like the north slope of Alaska and the North Sea. But the price collapse of the 1980's led to nearly two decades of oil over-supply that discouraged additional investments.

In recent years, oil executives say they have made discoveries in Angola, Nigeria, Libya, Kazakhstan and Algeria, to name a few countries. The industry hope is that increased exploration and more intensive efforts at existing oil fields will enable producers to expand output enough to keep up demand, preventing prices from soaring and sustaining economic growth around the world.

"There's still plenty of room to play here," Mr. O'Reilly said in an interview in Houston after his speech. "In the last decade, there's been more opening than closing. The pendulum swings in this business."

THE POLITICS
Ambitious Proposals Stuck in the Beltway

When Bill Clinton was campaigning in New Hampshire in early 1992, the cost of oil was very much on voters' minds. The economy was weak and the third energy scare of the late 20th century—Saddam Hussein's invasion of Kuwait in 1990, which shut down nearly 3.4 million barrels a day of crude oil output for nearly a year—was still a powerful memory. The last of the Kuwaiti wells set aflame by the retreating Iraqis had been put out only a few months earlier.

But by the time President Clinton took office in January 1993, the price of crude oil was much lower and falling.

Passing an energy bill was not on the administration's agenda, but putting one into practice was. Congress had approved an ambitious law in 1992 intended to promote alternatives to gasoline. The goal was for 10 percent of the vehicle fleet to be capable of running on something else by 2000; by 2010 it was supposed to be 30 percent.

Today, the number is still under 1 percent.

"We did the best we could under the circumstances," Mr. Clinton said in a recent interview, "but there was minimal interest, the economy was growing like crazy, there was no inflation and oil was cheap."

By 1994, the price of crude oil bottomed out at less than $16 a barrel, making it impossible to save money by switching to something else. Low gasoline prices, combined with a rapidly improving economy, brought an explosion in the number of vehicles, to nearly one per driver. Many more of the new vehicles were S.U.V.'s, pickup trucks and minivans, all gulping fuel.

As part of his deficit-reduction program, Mr. Clinton managed to push through an increase in the federal excise tax on gasoline to 18.4 cents a gallon, from 14.1 cents. But he had to abandon a much more ambitious proposal to raise energy taxes across the board as part of an effort to limit global warming and control pollution from fossil fuels.

"I hadn't run on it, and hadn't made any kind of foundation to do anything on it," Mr. Clinton said. "It was sprung on Congress," he added, sounding regretful.

Despite the retreat on energy taxes, the vote on the budget bill was still so close in the Senate that Vice President Al Gore had to cast the deciding vote. There was never any chance of achieving anything close to the taxes levied in Europe, where consumers pay up to $5 a gallon for gasoline, mostly due to taxes.

"In Europe, people are less dependent on cars, they use smaller cars, and a gas tax wasn't as controversial as it would be here," Mr. Clinton said.

The atmosphere for cutting oil consumption might be better now, he said, than it was during his tenure. "There is a lot greater awareness, even though we're moving away from 9/11, of our vulnerability," he said. "We've got to get a vehicle fleet that doesn't depend on oil as much."

But given political constraints, which block any serious effort at fuel efficiency or raising energy taxes, the government is stymied, according to Philip R. Sharp, a veteran of Washington's energy wars and an Indiana Democrat who served in Congress from 1975 to 1995.

"We cannot in any rapid fashion or cheap fashion have a radical impact," said Mr. Sharp, who drafted large parts of the 1992 energy bill that sought to wean the nation away from gasoline. "It is very hard for public policy makers to grasp how large this marketplace is. It's gigantic."

Japan Almost Doubles Forecast for Economic Growth

By TODD ZAUN—July 22, 2004

TOKYO, July 21—The Japanese government nearly doubled its forecast for the nation's economic growth to 3.5 percent for the year ending March 2005, the result of a sharp upturn in business investment and increased consumer spending.

The new outlook is in line with forecasts by private economists, and, if achieved, would be Japan's fastest growth since 1997, when the economy expanded 3.6 percent. The cabinet office of Prime Minister Junichiro Koizumi had previously forecast the economy would grow 1.8 percent in the current fiscal year.

The cabinet office also said, however, that it expected growth to slow to "slightly more than 2 percent" in the following fiscal year, which ends in March 2006. That forecast, too, is roughly in line with the views of private economists, most of whom expect Japan's expansion to decelerate as corporate investment slows and China's torrid economic growth continues to cool. Japan's economy is closely tied to China's, and therefore vulnerable to any slowdown there.

The government broke with tradition by offering a revision to its economic forecasts so early in the year, but after two quarters of surprisingly strong growth, the government's forecasts had begun to look unrealistically low. Generally, the cabinet office has released its economic forecasts in the fall. Wednesday was also the first time the office made projections for the following fiscal year.

Japan's gross domestic product grew at an annual rate of 6.1 percent for the quarter ended in March as consumer demand—the missing element from previous short-lived recoveries—rebounded, adding to already strong exports and business investment.

In its new forecast, the cabinet office said it expected rising business investment to continue to make a big contribution to overall economic growth. Capital investment by companies was expected to rise 9.9 percent in the current fiscal year, while consumer spending was anticipated to be up 2.6 percent.

"Amid a global economic recovery, the rise in production and capital investment continues and now is expected to broaden to the household sector," the cabinet office wrote in a brief report accompanying its forecasts.

The report forecast that government investment would shrink 12.5 percent for the fiscal year, in line with a promise by Mr. Koizumi's government to rein in the nation's growing budget deficit.

As Japan shows unexpected economic vitality, few economists seem to doubt the country will meet the growth estimates for the current fiscal year. And so, econo-mists are turning their attention to 2005.

Although consumer spending has recently begun to pick up, the main driver of Japan's two-year old economic recovery continues to be growth overseas, particularly in the United States and China. Strong demand for Japanese electronic goods, like cellphones, flat-panel televisions and DVD players, has driven an investment binge by manufacturers.

While business investment is expected to continue for much of the remainder of this year, many economists doubt it will last into 2005.

"We believe we are getting toward the end of the expansion," said Robert Feldman, chief economist for Morgan Stanley in Tokyo.

Also, any cooling in China's growth will curtail investment by Japanese companies that have been benefiting from China's rapid expansion in recent years, he added. For the Japanese economy, "the China component is going to slow down," said Mr. Feldman, who forecasts Japan's economy will slow to 0.9 percent in the 2005 fiscal year. "Even if there's a soft landing in China, it's a landing."

But Peter Morgan, an economist at HSBC Securities in Tokyo, said he did not believe that a slowdown in China would significantly hurt the Japanese economy. He argued that many of Japan's exports to China are components that are assembled in Chinese factories into goods bound for the United States and other markets. Therefore, he said, Japanese exports to China might remain relatively strong even if growth there slowed.

"The bulk of Japan's exports to China are being re-exported," Mr. Morgan said. The impact to Japan, therefore, "is probably not as big as most people are expecting."

Rich Nations Are Urged to Ease Trade With Affected Countries

By ELIZABETH BECKER—January 15, 2005

WASHINGTON, Jan. 14—The head of the World Trade Organization issued a plea to all member nations on Friday to lower trade barriers as a way of helping nations ravaged by the tsunami.

Supachai Panitchpakdi, the director general and a native of Thailand, asked countries to open up their markets to encourage a strong revival of the hard-hit economies. He also asked that members refrain from reprisals against the worst-hit economies for unfair trade practices.

"As someone from the affected region, I naturally feel a particular sense of tragedy," Mr. Supachai wrote in a letter to the members.

Although the W.T.O. is not involved in disaster relief, Mr. Supachai said the organization shared "part of the responsibility to assist recovery from the tsunami."

Calls for trade relief reflect the understanding that a country's ability to restore livelihoods may depend on selling products overseas. But as in previous tragedies, the appeals for trade concessions are being resisted by industries that could suffer from the resulting competition.

The United States and the European Union have already said they would consider suspending some of the duties imposed on products from the countries hardest hit. The European Union is also considering speeding up trade preferences that were scheduled for July.

Moreover, the European Union is sending experts to help repair damage to processing facilities and ensure that food prepared for export meets health standards.

"Food is a big export for these countries, so we're sending help to get them back up and running so they will be able to export again," said Anthony Gooch, a spokesman for the European Union in Washington. The United States is pushing to complete talks on trade and investment agreements with Thailand, Indonesia, Malaysia and Sri Lanka, said Richard Mills, spokesman for Robert B. Zoellick, the United States trade representative.

Some countries have already come up with their own ideas: Thailand, which has said it will rebuild on its own, is asking to be spared from new United States tariffs on shrimp. Sri Lanka wants special consideration for its textile exports.

With the end of the global multifiber agreement at the beginning of this year, the poorer countries of the region had already asked the United States for special consideration, especially in the face of the new competition they face with China.

Deborah Long, spokeswoman for the Southern Shrimp Alliance, said there were other ways to help than to suspend duties imposed last week on Asian and Latin American countries for selling shrimp at below market prices. A more equitable solution, she argued, was for American retailers to pay shrimpers higher prices.

Lloyd Woods, a spokesman for the American Manufacturing Trade Action Coalition, which represents most American textile companies, said the best way to help Sri Lanka, Thailand and India was to go ahead with proposed limits on Chinese imports, indirectly bolstering the competitiveness of the other nations.

Oxfam America wrote to Mr. Zoellick on Friday seeking preferences to Sri Lanka, the Maldives and Indonesia for textiles and clothing. Currently the United States gives such preferences to many nations in Central America, South America and sub-Saharan Africa.

Texas Lawmakers Meet, With Education Atop Agenda

By RALPH BLUMENTHAL—January 12, 2005

AUSTIN, Jan. 11—The second Tuesday of an odd year (and this year could be odder than most) brought Texas legislators streaming into town under the gun of a judge's order to fix a broken school financing system.

With the failure of last year's special legislative session to produce a solution, and emotions still raw over a strong-arm Republican redistricting that saw Democratic lawmakers leaving the state in protest, the state's 79th biennial legislative session could prove crucial to many political careers, experts say.

"It could go down as the most historic of modern times," Gov. Rick Perry told the 31 senators as he made unusual appearances for brief pep talks in both houses amid the pomp of opening day. Mr. Perry has been rounding up pledges of support from fellow Republicans for a re-election campaign in 2006.

But a stumble with school financing or another big issue could embolden such likely challengers in his own party as Senator Kay Bailey Hutchison and the state's comptroller, Carole Keeton Strayhorn, who have hinted that they are considering a run. Their candidacies would set off a scramble for their seats.

Ms. Strayhorn opened last year with news of a $10 billion budget shortfall, which was closed with the help of sharp cuts in social programs like children's insurance. This week, she had a happier prognosis: she forecast a $400 million surplus, only a blip compared with the state's projected $65 billion in revenues, but at least not red ink as long as cuts in social programs are not restored.

Finding a new way to support Texas's 4 million schoolchildren rocketed to the top of the lawmakers' agenda after Judge John Dietz of District Court ruled in September in a lawsuit by more than 300 school districts that the $30-billion-a-year financing system was unconstitutional.

The judge found that the so-called Robin Hood system, in which wealthier districts help underwrite poorer districts, did not generate enough money to meet statewide constitutional standards. He also found that although the state constitution forbids a statewide property tax, so many localities were at their maximum taxing power to support education that it was in effect a statewide property tax.

Judge Dietz gave state officials until October 2005 to come up with a new financing system or face a cutoff of all education financing. The state appealed to the Texas Supreme Court. But while hoping for a reversal, officials still vow to tackle the problem in the Legislature.

"Without doubt, the primary objective of this session and every session of the Legislature should be school funding," said Tom Craddick, Republican of Midland, who was overwhelmingly re-elected speaker of the 150-member House.

Mr. Craddick, an 18-term veteran who first took his seat as a 25-year-old in 1969, joked about shifting the blame. "One of the grievances of those who fought at the Alamo was Mexico's failure to establish a school system," he said. "We still have today the same problem. I just wanted to tell the people of Texas we didn't create the school problem. It started at the Alamo."

Where the schools money will come from is the overwhelming question. Texas has no state income tax, and one is not likely to be established by legislators who hope to keep their jobs. Amending the Constitution to allow a statewide property tax is also widely seen as political suicide. The state prides itself as being the most business-friendly in the nation, so new business taxes are likewise unpalatable.

"There's a reason this stuff is hard," wrote Paul Burka, political columnist for Texas Monthly magazine.

Although tax bills originate in the House, many political observers expect the first outline of a solution to emerge from the Senate under its presiding officer, Lt. Gov. David Dewhurst, a Republican who is sometimes mentioned as a candidate for governor in 2010, if not before.

The mood at the sand-colored Capitol, second largest after the nation's Capitol in Washington, was festive, with herds of schoolchildren filing into the galleries, family members of legislators snapping photos, cadres of lobbyists buttonholing lawmakers, and even an accordionist strolling the corridors. Prayers were said, and the national anthem and the state song were sung.

In an emotional ceremony, Melissa Noriega, the wife of a House member serving in Afghanistan, Rick Noriega, Democrat of Houston, was seated as his temporary replacement. It was the first application of a 2003 provision approved by the Legislature to allow members on active military duty to designate a substitute.

But tensions eventually surfaced. Supporters of Hubert Vo, a Vietnamese businessman from Houston who unseated a longtime Republican leader in November by 32 votes out of 40,000 cast, rallied on the steps to endorse his victory in the face of a challenge by his opponent, Talmadge Heflin, that is being heard by the Republican-dominated House.

Introducing his family to the crowd, Mr. Vo mentioned that his son had a black belt in karate. "Put him on Heflin," someone shouted.

U.S. to Permit Cattle Imports From Canada

By CLIFFORD KRAUSS—December 30, 2004

TORONTO, Dec. 29—The Bush administration announced Wednesday that it would permit limited imports of Canadian cattle early next year for the first time since May 2003, when a case of mad cow disease was discovered in an Alberta cow.

The Department of Agriculture's decision, to allow cattle under the age of 30 months to be imported beginning March 7, is likely to ease one of the most nettlesome trade disputes between Ottawa and Washington.

More than 6,000 Canadian jobs have been lost because of the ban, hurting Prime Minister Paul Martin politically in the western provinces.

Recognizing Canada as a "minimal risk region" for mad cow disease, bovine spongiform encephalopathy, Agriculture Secretary Ann M. Veneman said in a statement, "After conducting an extensive review, we are confident that imports of certain commodities from regions of minimal risk can occur with virtually no risk to human or animal health."

The rule change will also expand the variety of cuts of beef that can be imported from Canada.

Live cattle will only be able to enter the United States in sealed containers, and no breeding cattle will be allowed.

Nevertheless, Canadian cattlemen were excited by the news.

"Its good for business," said Ted Wood, co-owner of Weiller & Williams Ltd., a prominent Edmonton cattle brokerage and feeder. Although he cautioned that the falling American dollar and rising Canadian dollar would continue to slow export growth in the Canadian cattle industry, he added, "We'll be in a profitable area, which we haven't been in three years."

American Agriculture Department officials predicted that American feedlots would import two million head of cattle in the new year, which should lower prices of beef and beef products for American consumers.

The partial end of the ban comes as Canadian companies, prompted by fear that the ban would linger, are building meatpacking plants on the Canadian side of the border.

Those facilities, American diplomats in Ottawa said, could threaten profits of the American packing business in the future.

Plant Shortage Leaves Campaigns Against Malaria at Risk

By DONALD G. McNEIL Jr.—November 14, 2004

A Chinese herbal drug that is strikingly effective against malaria is in critically short supply because of rising demand, public health officials and pharmaceutical executives say.

As a result, prices for the drug, artemisinin, have quadrupled, and the few companies that make compounds containing it have drastically cut back production. Supply crises are looming in 40 tropical countries that have recently made it the centerpiece of their antimalarial efforts.

Malaria kills about one million people a year, most of them children. Strains resistant to older drugs have spread rapidly, and artemisinin (pronounced are-TEM-is-in-in), which is extracted from the sweet wormwood plant, was embraced this year by Western health agencies and donors as the most cost-effective solution.

The sudden shortage "has created a major wave of shock in our organization," said Dr. Andrea Bosman of the World Health Organization's malaria control team. Paul Lalvani, procurement manager for the Global Fund to Fight AIDS, Tuberculosis and Malaria, said the countries that had just adopted the drug were "really in a bind."

While other drugs are available, switching to a new one takes up to a year and can create dangerous confusion, especially in a poor country, he explained; the new drug must be registered, doctors and nurses must be retrained in dosages and side effects, and rural pharmacies must be alerted and restocked.

"Now they're sitting on the fence wondering if they should go ahead, or wait until the price drops, or pick another drug," he said.

Wormwood is an ancient Asian fever treatment, and Chinese military doctors trying to aid the Vietcong in the 1970's proved that its extracts kill malaria parasites. It has been popular in Southeast Asia, but was largely ignored in the West until this year.

Although sweet wormwood grows wild around the world, virtually all of the cultivation is in the hills of China and Vietnam.

Each crop must be planted in January, harvested in the fall, and then dried and processed. Some would-be growers outside China are complaining that they cannot buy seeds.

The shortage began soon after a series of meetings in April at which the Global Fund, the W.H.O., the World Bank, Unicef, the United States Agency for International Development and other donors jointly announced that they wanted malaria-prone countries to phase out older drugs like chloroquine and sulfadoxine-pyrimethamine and adopt multidrug combinations containing artemisinin or its derivatives artemether or artesunate.

Even though the new drugs cost 10 to 20 times as much, the donors chose them because resistance to older drugs was running as high as 60 percent in parts of Africa. (A typical adult course of 24 of the newer pills costs the W.H.O. $2.40, as against 20 cents for chloroquine.)

Until early this year, the world consumed about 30 tons of raw artemisinin a year, mostly in Asia, and the price had been steady for several years at about $115 a pound.

But immediately after the W.H.O.'s April forecast that the world would need 130 to 220 tons in 2005, the price rose to $180 a pound. It is now $365 to $455 a pound.

Drug companies in Switzerland and India say they cannot get enough at any price, and blame is being directed at all corners.

Mr. Lalvani, the Global Fund procurement specialist, said the refiners stopped selling this summer, "waiting for the prices to stabilize or go higher."

Pradeep Nambiar, an executive at Ipca Laboratories, an Indian company, said that its Chinese suppliers had reneged on contracts and that he believed they could be "holding back stock anticipating a price rise."

The most vivid evidence of the shortage emerged last Monday, when Novartis, a major Swiss drug company, said it could produce only about half of the 4.5 million courses of its Co-Artem drug that it had promised to deliver to the W.H.O. by March. Its lone artemisinin supplier in China had fallen short, it said.

Co-Artem is the only malaria drug prequalified by the W.H.O., an endorsement of its safety. It also combines two drugs in one pill, making it harder for a patient to give away or sell part of a dose.

As a result, many poor countries, encouraged by donors and Novartis, specifically adopted Co-Artem. Now some, like Zambia and Ethiopia, will have their supplies rationed.

Novartis has a 10-year contract to make its "reasonable best effort" to supply, at cost, all the Co-Artem the W.H.O. asks for. It had made a commitment to deliver 60 million doses by the end of 2005, but even its relatively small first batch will fall short.

Daniel Berman, a campaigner for lower drug prices at the medical charity Doctors Without Borders, criticized Novartis, saying it had underestimated how much raw material it would need and had relied on one supplier. Daniela Currie, a Novartis spokeswoman, said the W.H.O. had made its forecast only after the 2004 crop was in the ground and some planned extraction plants were still not built. "These are things we can't really influence," she said, adding that Novartis has now found two more suppliers.

She said she had "no evidence" that the company's Chinese suppliers, who also make drugs that compete with Co-Artem, had cut it off in hopes of taking some of its market share now that the W.H.O. is under pressure to prequalify more drugs.

In conversations with visiting experts from two Western public health agencies, summaries of which were obtained by The New York Times, executives from several Chinese artemisinin refiners blamed their own suppliers for the sudden rise in prices. After the April meetings, they said, the word spread in China that the West wanted the drug.

Because of the artemisinin shortage, the W.H.O. now ranks several pills made in India and China that combine artemisinin with other drugs like amodiaquine and mefloquine as "approved for procurement in the absence of prequalified product."

Plans are also afoot to grow wormwood in India, Tanzania and southern Africa. Some farmers have had trouble getting potent seeds, but Mr. Nambiar said Ipca had stockpiled them.

Mr. Lalvani said he was worried.

"For 2005, we're stuck," he said. "But let's not be stuck for the year after that. We need to come up with a solution for this—and right away."

In Brazil, Sugar Cane Growers Become Fuel Farmers

By TODD BENSON—May 24, 2005

CATANDUVA, Brazil—Not long ago, residents of this lush cane-growing region in southern Brazil needed to keep a close eye on the price of sugar in world markets to know if the local farmers were hiring or firing.

These days, however, most people in this small farming town seem more preoccupied with the price of oil. And with good reason. Ever since global oil prices started their staggering climb early last year, demand for inexpensive alternative fuels like cane-based ethanol has skyrocketed, helping to line the pockets of Brazilian cane farmers while also making them less vulnerable to the swings of the sugar market.

"Ethanol is on its way to becoming a commodity just like oil, and the price of oil is one of the main reasons why," said José Fernandes Rio, a director at Usina Cerradinho, one of eight sugar mills and ethanol distilleries scattered around Catanduva, which is spending heavily to increase production.

The growing demand for ethanol—or alcohol, as most Brazilians call it—is fueling an investment boom in Brazil's sugar cane industry not seen since the oil crisis of the 1970's.

Back then, the country's military dictatorship sought to reduce dependence on costly foreign oil by offering lavish subsidies and tax breaks to sugar millers to refine cane into ethanol, while also financing the construction of a nationwide distribution network for the fuel.

Though oil jitters are once again helping to drive the current wave of investment in Brazil's sugar industry, this time the government is not picking up the bill. Flush with cash from a recovery in global sugar prices in recent years, many millers are spending their own money and borrowing from banks to increase production and upgrade port terminals, mills and distilleries to improve service to foreign markets.

According to a recent survey by ProCana, a research group in Ribeirão Preto that tracks the sugar and ethanol industry, 12.5 billion reais ($5.1 billion) has already been earmarked for 40 new mills and distilleries over the next five years. Most of that money will be spent here in western São Paulo State, a region that is already home to dozens of sugar mills, generating close to 100,000 jobs in an industry that employs more than a million people.

"Of all the different investment waves that the industry has had, this is clearly the most solid one of all," said Maurílio Biagi Filho, an executive at CrystalSev, a large sugar and ethanol conglomerate that is putting the finishing touches on a $10 million ethanol terminal at the port of Santos.

"People have money to invest, and both domestic and external demand is on the rise," added Mr. Biagi, whose family has been in the sugar business since 1920. "All the ingredients are there."

Not long ago, ethanol's future did not look so bright. In the heyday of the government's pro-alcohol campaign in the mid-1980's, ethanol-only cars accounted for almost 90 percent of new-auto sales in Brazil. But domestic ethanol consumption started declining steadily in 1990, when a poor cane harvest and high sugar prices caused an alcohol shortage that enraged drivers, prompting many to switch back to cars powered by gasoline.

Then, three years ago, Volkswagen began selling cars in Brazil that run on either gasoline or ethanol, or any combination of the two. Lured by the low cost of alcohol—it sells for almost half the price of gasoline—Brazilians have been buying these so-called flex-fuel cars in droves, helping to revive the domestic ethanol market.

Today, all major automakers in Brazil offer these hybrid vehicles, which now represent 33 percent of new-car sales, a figure that some analysts predict could reach 80 percent by the end of next year.

Thanks to the popularity of flex-fuel engines, domestic ethanol consumption is expected to jump 50 percent in the next five years, meaning that a growing percentage of the country's annual cane crop will be used to make fuel. This season, for example, a record 57 percent of the harvest is expected to go to ethanol production, up from less than half in recent years, according to Datagro, a sugar and ethanol consulting firm based in São Paulo.

"People used to say that our only chance to sell more ethanol was to increase exports," said Eduardo Pereira de Carvalho, president of Unica, the country's largest association of sugar and ethanol producers. "That changed overnight with flex-fuel cars."

Because no other country has an ethanol distribution network as extensive as Brazil's, it is unlikely that flex-fuel cars will become an international trend any time soon. But with world oil prices hovering around $50 a barrel, governments around the globe are looking for ways to replace gasoline with ethanol.

Almost a dozen countries, including Canada, Sweden and the United States, have already begun blending ethanol with gasoline, a practice that has been mandatory in Brazil for years. This helps keep a lid on prices at the pump while also reducing fuel emissions, a requirement for nations that signed environmental treaties like the Kyoto Protocol.

Other countries, like Australia and Thailand, are turning to Brazil for help to develop their own ethanol industries to feed demand for affordable energy in Asia, especially from China. India, the world's No. 2 sugar producer after Brazil, is also scrambling to spread the use of ethanol to reduce its reliance on foreign oil as its auto fleet expands along with its middle class.

For now, Brazil, with its low production costs, plentiful land and well-established ethanol industry, is benefiting the most. Last year alone, for instance, its ethanol exports tripled to almost $500 million as oil prices soared, with the United States and India topping the list of importers.

And as pressure mounts on the European Union to comply with the World Trade Organization's order that it do away with sugar subsidies, making sugar production less profitable there, more foreign sugar producers and trading houses are likely to set their sights on Brazil to keep their businesses alive.

Theo Spettman, chief executive of Südzucker of Germany, Europe's biggest sugar producer, said at a seminar this month in São Paulo that the company was looking for investment opportunities in Brazil. If it takes the plunge, Südzucker will follow in the footsteps of French companies like Louis Dreyfus, Tereos and Sucden. All set up shop in Brazil in recent years.

"The big players in the sugar industry in Europe are not going to stop being big just because their subsidies are going to end," said Josias Messias, president of ProCana, the research group that studies sugar and ethanol.

"They know they're going to have to invest here."

To Reduce the Cost of Teenage Temptation, Why Not Just Raise the Price of Sin?

By DAVID LEONHARDT—July 25, 2005

WHEN you look back on all the attempts to curb teenage drinking, smoking and drug use over the last couple of decades, you start to ask yourself a question that countless parents have asked: Does anybody really know how to change a teenager's behavior?

Sometimes the government and advocacy groups have used straight talk, like Nancy Reagan's "Just Say No" campaign. Other times they have tried to play it cool. They drop an egg into a sizzling frying pan and announce, "This is your brain on drugs," or they print mock advertisements that pretend to market cancer. It all feels like a delicate exercise in adolescent psychology.

Much of this back and forth is unnecessary. There is in fact a sure-fire way to get teenagers to consume less beer, tobacco and drugs, according to one study after another: raise the cost, in terms of either dollars or potential punishment.

In just about every state that increased beer taxes in recent years, teenage drinking soon dropped. The same happened in the early 1990's when Arizona, Maryland, New Jersey and a handful of other states passed zero-tolerance laws, which suspend the licenses of under-21 drivers who have any trace of alcohol in their blood. In states that waited until the late 90's to adopt zero tolerance, like Colorado, Indiana and South Carolina, the decline generally did not happen until after the law was in place.

Teenagers, it turns out, are highly rational creatures in some ways. Budweisers and Marlboros are discretionary items, and their customers treat them as such. Gasoline consumption, by contrast, changes only marginally when the price of a gallon does.

"When people think about drugs, alcohol, even cigarettes, they think about addiction and this strong desire to consume them. They don't think price has an effect," said Sara Markowitz, an economist at Rutgers University in Newark, who studies public health. "That's just wrong. And it holds among kids even more so than among adults."

Not only that, but unprotected sex tended to become less common after the changes in the law, according to studies. Gonorrhea and H.I.V. rates dropped. So did drunken-driving deaths and, for boys, suicides. Whatever the policies' downsides—and they are not insignificant—they have some of the clearest benefits of any government action.

They are also a useful reminder of how often the power of incentives is underestimated. Taste, style, trendiness and advertising all do affect human behavior. A study in the Archives of Pediatric and Adolescent Medicine this month, for example, found that antitobacco television ads do seem to reduce smoking. But nothing has quite the sway that an economic carrot or stick does.

When a big superstore moves into town, many shoppers who claim to prefer the coziness of mom-and-pop stores trek out to the megamall for the lower prices. (You know who you are.) When the government cut welfare payments in the 1990's, many people who had been receiving them went back to work.

Even when inscrutable teenagers and addictive substances are involved, the basic dynamic does not change.

Tax increases on alcohol and tobacco have been fairly common in recent years, allowing researchers to look for the crucial before-and-after effect that helps separate correlation from causation. Alaska, Nebraska, Nevada, Tennessee and Utah have all increased alcohol taxes since 2002. Georgia, Kentucky, Tennessee and Virginia—tobacco-growing states all—are among those that have raised cigarette taxes.

Just because states with higher taxes have lower teenage drinking and smoking rates does not mean that one caused the other. An outside force—like a highly educated population, which might tend to eschew beer and cigarettes but vote for higher taxes—could instead be the underlying cause.

But if drinking or smoking always seems to fall after a tax increase, then the case becomes far stronger. Looking across the states and taking into account all the other factors that can be measured, researchers have found that a 1 percent increase in the price of beer leads to a drop in teenage consumption of between 1 and 4 percent, Dr. Markowitz said. For cigarettes, a 1 percent price increase causes roughly a 1 percent decline in smoking.

Using the same method, researchers can also answer a question that has long occupied public health specialists. It is generally accepted that youngsters who drink, smoke and use drugs are also more likely to take dangerous risks, like having unprotected sex. But does one lead to the other? Or as Christopher Carpenter, an economist at the University of California, Irvine, puts it, are there simply "bad kids" given to misbehaving in all sorts of ways?

Depending on your definition of misbehavior, the answer is both. When alcohol taxes rose, the number of teenagers who reported having had sex in recent months did not change, according to a study by Michael Grossman of the City University of New York and Dr. Markowitz. Nor did the number of partners they had.

But fewer teenagers had unprotected sex. The number of new gonorrhea cases and—though the evidence on this was weaker—new H.I.V. cases also dropped. Since teenagers get these diseases at far higher rates than the rest of the population, any decline can be a big deal.

The enactment of zero-tolerance driving laws also appeared to lead to a fall in sexually transmitted diseases. For boys between the ages of 15 and 20, suicide rates fell 7 percent to 10 percent after a law was put in place, Dr. Carpenter found. (The fact that the effects seem to be concentrated among boys and whites is a mystery that awaits future research.)

"When zero-tolerance laws were being debated, it wasn't like, 'Let's reduce drunk-driving deaths—and gonorrhea and suicide,' " he said. "This is an unintended, surprising consequence."

Zero-tolerance laws also have the advantage of being aimed specifically at teenagers. New alcohol taxes, on the other hand, take money from millions of people who do not spread venereal diseases or drive drunk.

But zero tolerance is now the law of the land in all 50 states, Dr. Carpenter said. There is no more public health uptick to get from it. So until somebody comes up with a smart new incentive, another "Don't Drink and Drive" campaign might be the best tool out there.

Parsing California Gas Prices

By HAL R. VARIAN—July 01, 2004

GASOLINE prices have finally started to fall, with the United States average declining by over 13 percent in the last month.

But California has not been as fortunate as the rest of the country. Prices there are down only 8 cents, and remain the highest in the continental United States.

Why did gas prices go up so sharply in the spring? Why did they subsequently decline? And why do California gasoline prices stay so stubbornly high?

May's surge has been widely attributed to a fear of oil supply disruptions in the Middle East. Skeptics have argued that the possibility of future disruptions should not affect current prices. After all, they argue, the oil used to manufacture the gasoline now being sold at the pump has already been bought and paid for.

But this economic analysis is flawed. Gasoline is easy to store, so if the price is expected to increase, refiners and shippers will keep more in storage, in anticipation of those higher prices. The resulting reduction in current supply will push prices up now, before any actual shortages materialize.

That's the way the market should work. If you believed that gasoline would become scarcer in a few weeks, wouldn't you want to economize on use now to ensure a larger supply in the future?

Luckily, the feared disruptions have not occurred (yet), and prices began to fall at the end of May. In addition to the reduction in worries about oil supply disruptions and the increased oil production from OPEC, increased gasoline imports, particularly from Venezuela, helped drive down prices. According to the Automobile Club of Southern California, "International refiners are like the cavalry, riding to the rescue of overcharged motorists."

Maybe so, but Californians are still getting trampled. Prices in California are 30 cents higher than the national average and much more volatile.

The economics of the California gasoline market are described in a recent study by Severin Borenstein, James Bushnell and Matthew Lewis of the University of California Energy Institute (http://www.ucei.org/PDF/csemwp132.pdf).

The basic problem comes down to supply and demand. California uses a special low-polluting blend of gasoline known as CaRFG (California reformulated gasoline), which is produced by only 13 in-state refineries. In 2003 these refineries produced about 15 billion gallons, a figure almost identical to the 14.8 billion gallons consumed in the state.

California's production capacity is so closely matched to its demand that even sharp increases in price result in little additional production of gasoline.

On the other side of the market, the demand for gasoline is also quite insensitive to price: a 10 percent increase in price typically reduces short-term demand by only 2 to 3 percent.

The result is that even small fluctuations in the demand or supply of CaRFG can lead to large price swings.

The market forces of supply and demand offer a reasonably convincing explanation as to why the California gasoline market is so volatile. But this may not be the entire story.

The market is controlled by seven large suppliers, ranging from ChevronTexaco, with a 27 percent share, down to Exxon Mobil, which supplies 8 percent of the market. With only seven suppliers, price manipulation may also be at work.

When demand is insensitive to price and capacity is more or less fixed, sellers have mixed incentives. When prices rise, a refiner can make an immediate profit by selling more gasoline; if all suppliers sell more, the price is pushed back down. But if a few large companies withhold gasoline supplies, they can keep the price propped up for an extended period.

The authors of the report are quick to point out that they have no evidence that this has occurred. Indeed, they argue that the basic economics of the industry make it difficult to find such evidence in price and quantity movements alone.

However, they also point out that the temptation to manipulate price is certainly present, and a prudent response from Sacramento would be to enact policies that will reduce that temptation as much as possible.

It is important to recognize that it is not illegal under American antitrust laws for a supplier to withhold gasoline or any other commodity. Individual energy companies are free to produce or not produce, store or not store, as they see fit. That is the nature of a free market.

It is illegal for companies to collude to create an artificial scarcity, but collusion is extremely hard to prove.

The California economists examine various policy responses that might help reduce price volatility and mitigate the incentives to exercise market power: maintaining a strategic fuel reserve, regulating seasonal changes in gasoline mix, regulating refinery closures and using state gasoline purchases more strategically.

All these proposals have serious problems. Heavy-handed regulation can easily make supply problems worse rather than better. The goal of policy should be not to displace markets, but to make them work better.

There is one market-based measure that shows considerable promise. This is to allow the importation of non-CaRFG gasoline into the state when CaRFG is in short supply, as long as the importer pays a tax equal to the difference in cost between CaRFG and non-CaRFG (about 15 cents a gallon).

When prices in California rise, sellers would then want to import gasoline from out of state, dampening the price increase. Air pollution might go up slightly for a few weeks, but the revenue from the gas tax could be used to finance other environmental measures, like buying back old, polluting cars.

Not only would this measure help dampen price fluctuations, it would also greatly reduce the temptation to manipulate prices—since any attempt to push up the price would be met with a flood of imported gasoline. Regardless of whether you believe price spikes result from market forces or market manipulation, increasing gasoline supply when prices rise has got to be a good thing for Californians.

Hal R. Varian is a professor of business, economics and information management at the University of California, Berkeley.

New Jersey Faces Pressure to Increase Gas Tax

By DAVID KOCIENIEWSKI—February 07, 2005

TRENTON, Feb. 4—As New Jersey residents and elected officials brace themselves for an ugly budget season of deficits, spending cuts and tax increases, another problem is looming in the background: growing pressure to raise its gasoline tax this year.

The Transportation Trust Fund, which uses the state's 14.5 cent-per-gallon gas tax to build and maintain New Jersey's overloaded system of roads, bridges and rail lines, is expected to run out of money in June 2006. During the past five years, a succession of governors and legislative leaders from both parties have considered—and scuttled—plans to replenish the fund either by increasing the gas tax or by devoting revenues from other parts of the budget.

But with the fund teetering toward insolvency, state officials must find a solution or risk losing $1 billion in federal transportation aid that is allocated to match state contributions. All those years of deferring the problem mean that by next year, New Jersey drivers could face sticker shock at the gas pump: as much as a 15-cent-per-gallon increase proposed by some transportation experts and commuters groups.

Acting Gov. Richard J. Codey has said that he is willing to consider the matter later this year, after he wrangles with the estimated $4 billion budget shortfall this spring and the General Assembly elections in November. Meanwhile, an assortment of business leaders, lawmakers, labor groups and commuters organizations are working on a plan to win public support for the tax, which has been opposed by as many as 70 percent of voters in recent polls.

Even those pushing for a plan to replenish the Transportation Trust Fund concede that it may be tricky to sell to New Jersey drivers. Many New Jersey residents are notoriously emotional about their cars and do not want to pay any more to drive. The state's current gas tax, one of the lowest in the nation, is also partly responsible for making New Jersey's gasoline prices lower than other states in the region.

"I think the only way you can convince people is by assuring them that any tax increase will be used for the purposes it is intended and will make their daily lives better by improving their commutes and their roads," said Philip K. Beachem, head of the New Jersey Alliance for Action, which is sponsoring a conference to rally support for the transportation fund on Monday in Trenton.

The fund was established in 1984 and devised to prevent lawmakers from diverting the gas tax to nontransportation purposes. The idea was to create a pay-as-you-go system and dedicate gas taxes for road, bridge and mass transit projects, using a limited amount of borrowing for major capital expenses. Since 1990, however, the fund has relied so heavily on borrowing that this year it devoted nearly two-thirds of its budget to debt service. By 2006, its entire $805 million budget would be needed to pay off loans.

Martin Robbins, a Rutgers professor who analyzes transportation systems, said the borrowing paid for a Christmas list of major transportation improvements. A few projects, like the Camden-Trenton light rail line, have been criticized as a questionable use of public money. But Mr. Robbins said that many of the projects have provided upgrades to New Jersey's transportation infrastructure, including the Hudson-Bergen light rail line, subsidies for New Jersey Transit riders, rail stations in Montclair and at Newark Liberty International Airport, the rail transfer station in Secaucus and a variety of road improvements.

But the state now must pay back the bonds used to fund those projects, and the bill will be steep. A blue ribbon commission created by former Gov. James E. McGreevey in 2003 said that the state's infrastructure was deteriorating so rapidly that the state needed to increase the tax by 12.5 cents per gallon to raise the hundreds of millions of dollars needed to finance the necessary maintenance work. Mr. McGreevey then surprised lawmakers by scrapping the idea of an increase completely, saying it would undermine the state's fragile economic recovery.

Since then, however, the situation has grown more pressing. The Bush administration appears unlikely to provide $125 million a year in additional transportation aid the state had been expecting, and more cuts in federal aid appear to be likely this year. Assemblyman John S. Wisniewski, chairman of the Transportation Committee, said that the state risks hurting its business climate if it allows its over-stressed transportation system to further deteriorate.

"Every day we see gridlock, roads that aren't repaved, mass transit that doesn't serve drivers as well as it should," said Mr. Wisniewski, a Democrat from Middlesex County. "New Jersey's whole economy is so dependent on having a functional infrastructure that if we don't invest in that economic engine, we're going to hurt our selves and be worse off in the long run."

Mr. Wisniewski and Assemblyman Peter J. Biondi, a Republican from Hillsborough, have sponsored a bill that prevent the state from spending more than 50 percent of its transportation fund on debt service. Despite those provisions, the state's ranking Republican, Leonard Lance, the Senate minority leader, expressed skepticism about the plan. But even some groups that advocate on behalf of drivers seem resigned to some tax increase being imposed.

"We have to be certain that drivers are treated fairly," said Pam Maiolo, president of public affairs of the Mid-Atlantic American Automobile Association. "But the state clearly needs some sort of long-term solution. It just can't put it off any longer."

Europe's Plan on Subsidies Aims to Cut Sugar Prices

By GRAHAM BOWLEY—June 23, 2005
International Herald Tribune

BRUSSELS, June 22—The European Commission on Wednesday announced a plan to overhaul its sugar subsidy system that would cut prices by 39 percent. If approved, the proposal could lead to wide-ranging job cuts and a big drop in production.

Big sugar users in the food and beverage industry welcomed the proposed changes to the system, which has kept prices paid by European consumers at levels three times that on world markets.

The changes met with an immediate wave of protest from developing countries that export sugar to Europe at the higher prices and that are afraid the reductions would devastate their domestic industries.

Consumer groups also expressed concern about the proposal, saying that it would lead to reduced competition by forcing smaller producers out of business.

"As a result, consumers may enjoy little if any benefits in terms of lower sugar prices," Jim Murray, director of the European Consumers' Organization, said in a statement.

Mariann Fischer Boel, the European Commission agriculture commissioner, said, however, that changes were needed to modernize a system that has remained largely untouched since it began nearly 40 years ago.

"If we did nothing, then Europe's sugar industry would suffer a long and painful death," she said.

If the changes are made, she said, "We will be able to guarantee a viable and sustainable long-term future for Europe's sugar producers."

Europe produces nearly 20 million tons of sugar a year, making it the third-largest sugar producer after Brazil and India.

The commission said the changes would bring the European sugar industry into line with other areas of agriculture, including cereals and dairy products, where subsidies have been overhauled in the last few years.

Ms. Fischer Boel said farmers forced out of sugar production would be given aid to help them diversify into new areas.

The commission also announced a 2006 aid package of 40 million euros for some countries in Africa and in the Caribbean and Pacific regions that rely on high sugar prices in Europe. But those countries denounced the aid as inadequate and called for a more gradual reduction in sugar prices.

"This proposal in its current form will badly hurt some of the poorest countries in the world," said Luis Morago, a spokesman for Oxfam International, a nongovernmental group involved in world poverty issues. "They won't get the investment desperately needed to build up their sugar sectors over the long term because," he said, the price cut is "too steep."

Big sugar users said the price cut did not go far enough and warned that some big commercial producers could still tacitly collude to keep prices high even after the support system was reduced.

Alain Beaumont, secretary general of CIUS, which represents sugar users like Coca-Cola and Heinz, said: "We believe it is a real opportunity to increase competition in the sugar industry. But the price cut is a minimum."

The proposals will dismantle a system that was put in place in 1968 and that protects E.U. sugar producers through a generous system of export subsidies, quotas and tariffs to block imports. It also buys sugar from farmers and processors at guaranteed prices.

The Dropout Puzzle

By PAUL KRUGMAN—July 18, 2005

MANY seemingly authoritative figures, not all of them partisan shills, say that the American economy has fully recovered from the recession that began in 2001. They point to the unemployment rate, which has fallen from a peak of 6.3 percent in 2003 to 5 percent last month. That's not quite as low as the 4.2 percent unemployment rate in February 2001, when the recession began, but it's fairly low by historical standards.

For some reason, however, the public isn't feeling prosperous. Gallup tells us that only 3 percent of Americans describe the economy as "excellent," and only 33 percent describe it as "good."

Maybe people are just ungrateful. Maybe they've been misled by negative media reports. Maybe they're grumpy about their paychecks: adjusted for inflation, average weekly earnings have been flat for the past five years.

Or maybe the figures on unemployment are giving a false signal.

Economists who argue that there's something wrong with the unemployment numbers are buzzing about a new study by Katharine Bradbury, an economist at the Federal Reserve Bank of Boston, which suggests that millions of Americans who should be in the labor force aren't. "The addition of these hypothetical participants," she writes, "would raise the unemployment rate by one to three-plus percentage points."

Some background: the unemployment rate is only one of several numbers economists use to assess the jobs picture. When the economy is generating an abundance of jobs, economists expect to see strong growth in the payrolls reported by employers and in the number of people who say they have jobs, together with a rise in the length of the average workweek. They also expect to see wage gains well in excess of inflation, as employers compete to attract workers.

In fact, we see none of these things. As Berkeley's J. Bradford DeLong writes on his influential economics blog, "We have four of five indicators telling us that the state of the job market is not that good and only one—the unemployment rate—reading green."

In particular, even the most favorable measures show that employment growth has lagged well behind population growth over the past four years. Yet the measured unemployment rate isn't much higher than it was in early 2001. How is that possible?

The answer, according to the survey used to estimate the unemployment rate, is a decline in labor force participation. Nonworking Americans aren't considered unemployed unless they are actively looking for work, and hence counted as part of the labor force. And a large number of people have, for some reason, dropped out of the official labor force.

Those with a downbeat view of the jobs picture argue that the low reported unemployment rate is a statistical illusion, that there are millions of Americans who would be looking for jobs if more jobs were available. Those with an upbeat view argue that labor force participation has fallen for reasons that have nothing to do with job availability—for example, young adults, recognizing the importance of education, may have chosen to stay in school longer.

That's where Dr. Bradbury's study comes in. She shows that the upbeat view doesn't hold up in the face of a careful examination of the numbers. In fact, because older Americans, especially older women, are more likely to work than in the past, labor force participation should have risen, not fallen, over the past four years. As a result, she suggests that there may be "considerable slack in the U.S. labor market": there are at least 1.6 million and possibly as many as 5.1 million people who aren't counted as unemployed but would take jobs if they were available.

There's both good news and bad news in that assessment. The good news is that the economy probably has plenty of room to expand before inflation becomes a problem (which implies that the Fed's decision to start raising interest rates was premature).

The bad news is that it's hard to see where further expansion will come from. We've already had four years of extremely loose fiscal and monetary policy. Tax cuts have pushed the federal budget deep into the red. Low interest rates have helped generate a housing bubble that has lifted real estate prices to ludicrous heights in major parts of the country.

If all that wasn't enough to give us a full economic recovery, what will?

E-mail: krugman@nytimes.com

German Unemployment Reaches 12.6%

By CARTER DOUGHERTY—March 02, 2005
International Herald Tribune

FRANKFURT, March 1—Unemployment in Germany, which crossed above the politically charged five million mark in January, rose again in February, to a rate of 12.6 percent with 5.2 million people out of work, the Federal Labor Agency said on Tuesday.

The unemployment rate, the highest since World War II, rose from 12.1 percent in January. Germany's economy has slumped recently, contracting 0.2 percent in the fourth quarter.

A bitterly cold winter put an unusually large number of construction employees out of work, but another reason for the high numbers was a statistical change to now count able-bodied recipients of social welfare payments as unemployed.

"As expected, the number of registered unemployed again rose markedly in February," Frank-Jürgen Wiese, the head of the Federal Labor Agency, said in a statement.

Chancellor Gerhard Schröder battled last year to pass the most thorough overhaul of unemployment benefits in decades, and the changes took effect on Jan. 1. Joblessness has risen since, and Mr. Schröder's Social Democrats face a crucial state election in May.

On May 22, the western state of North Rhine-Westphalia, the country's largest by population and home to 1.1 million unemployed, will decide whether to return a coalition of Social Democrats and the Green Party to power. The German political establishment widely views the polls as a dress rehearsal for federal elections in late 2006, when Mr. Schröder will seek a third term as chancellor.

Seasonal variations, which occur in areas like farming and construction that lay off workers in the winter, could bring Mr. Schröder's government some relief, said Andreas Rees, an economist with the HVB Group in Munich. "We see a lot of signs that the worst is behind us," Mr. Rees said.

In past years, seasonal unemployment has peaked in February, so by March an additional 150,000 people could be on the payrolls. If the trend continued, April's figures, which would be reported only a few weeks before the election, could bring unemployment well below five million, Mr. Rees noted.

The coming months will give some indication on another aspect of Mr. Schröder's changes, economists said. As a complement to greatly reduced unemployment benefits, able-bodied Germans who have been unemployed for more than a year will have to participate in municipal work programs.

Once they take these jobs, which could be cleaning up a park or working in a nursing home, they would be removed from the unemployment statistics—brightening the picture considerably.

Price Index Rose 3.3% in '04, Highest in 4 Years

By LOUIS UCHITELLE—January 20, 2005

THE Consumer Price Index, the best-known measure of inflation in America, rose 3.3 percent last year, the largest increase since 2000, the government reported yesterday.

The higher inflation rate was a result of a surge in oil prices early last year. Oil prices have since leveled off, allowing the inflation rate to return to more modest levels.

The moderating trend was already evident in December, when the index fell by 0.1 of a percent, the first month-to-month decline since July. That was mostly because of a sharp drop in gasoline prices; gas prices fell again in early January.

"We don't see any sign of an immediate pickup in inflation," said Andrew Tilton, an economist at Goldman Sachs, the Wall Street investment firm. "That said, looking out toward the end of the year, we think the trends are in the direction of a very modest pickup."

In the New York region, rising fuel costs helped drive the largest year-over-year increase in the index since 1990. [Page B1.]

The trends that Mr. Tilton and other forecasters point to are higher prices for imports as the dollar falls and for materials used in manufacturing.

Ian C. Shepherdson, chief economist for High Frequency Economics, said, "I think there will be a recognition, that if the dollar falls far enough and commodity prices rise fast enough, you can push up goods prices."

Citing such pressures, many Wall Street economists predicted yesterday that the Federal Reserve's policy makers would continue to raise interest rates by a quarter of a point at their meetings this year until the crucial federal funds rate gets at least above 3 percent and perhaps above 3.5 percent.

The federal funds rate, now at 2.25 percent, is the rate that banks and other financial institutions charge each other for loans. As it rises, so do mortgage and auto loan rates, as well as the cost of other consumer and business credit. The Fed's goal is to curtail spending and, in doing so, damp price increases.

Whatever the future holds, inflation today remains decidedly modest. The so-called core inflation rate, covering all prices except those for energy and food, rose 2.2 percent last year, roughly the rate that has prevailed each year since 1997 with the exception of 2003, when the core rate was 1.1 percent. The December increase conformed to this pattern; the core rose only 0.1 percent.

Rising prices for new and used cars accounted for more than half of the rise in last year's core C.P.I. rate, the Bureau of Labor Statistics reported. Actually, car prices rose only modestly, but they fell in 2003 and the swing from negative to positive magnified that category's contribution to inflation.

The swing drew a cautionary comment from Mr. Shepherdson. "The automakers are sneaking through sticker price increases and consumers are not feeling them because they are getting financing incentives," he said. "I guess what the manufacturers are hoping to do is reduce the incentives and reap the benefits of higher sticker prices."

The rising cost of housing and rates for hotel rooms also contributed significantly to last year's inflation rate. The various costs of maintaining a home rose most sharply, but hotel rates also jumped as travel picked up strongly.

Beyond the increases for autos and housing, and a noticeable rise in the prices of home furnishings and medical care, there was little upward movement in the prices of goods and services. Apparel prices fell in December, by 0.4 percent.

"The core inflation rate, in the broad historical scheme of things, is still very low, just over 2 percent," said Mark Zandi, chief economist at Economy.com, "and it is not likely to go much higher as long as the job market remains soft and there is still more production capacity in manufacturing than there is demand for what is produced."

The 3.3 percent jump in the overall inflation rate last year was the largest since 1991, except for the 3.4 percent rise in 2000. The rise in the average hourly wage last year did not keep pace, so workers lost ground. Real hourly wages, adjusted for inflation, fell 0.4 percent, the first decline since the early 1990's.

Separately, the Commerce Department reported that housing starts, when ground is broken for the construction of new homes and apartments, rose in December to a strong annual rate just above 2 million from 1.8 million, nearly as strong, in November. For all of last year, starts totaled 1.95 million.

After Years, Hong Kong Sees Return of Inflation

By KEITH BRADSHER—August 24, 2004

HONG KONG, Aug. 23—After five years and eight months of steadily falling prices that dragged down salaries and destroyed the value of many apartments, inflation has finally returned here, government statisticians announced on Monday.

The consumer price index edged up 0.9 percent in July compared with figures a year earlier, ending 68 consecutive months of decline. In June, prices had been 0.1 percent lower than a year earlier.

Ma Jun, an economist at Deutsche Bank, said rising prices in China were starting to pull up prices in Hong Kong, an autonomous Chinese territory that buys much of its food and goods from the mainland.

"Chinese inflation is now being exported to Hong Kong," he said.

Yet not everyone is benefiting. At a bustling outdoor market along a steep street of cut stones, stall keepers were unimpressed this afternoon by the government's announcement of an end to deflation.

"Actually, the situation is still getting worse," said Benny Sze, whose stall was filled with hundreds of spools of thread in a rainbow of brilliant hues. Clothing design shops and factories continue to move to the mainland, he explained.

Unemployment is still high, at 6.9 percent. Government statisticians classify an additional 3.5 percent of the labor force as underemployed, meaning that they are in part-time jobs because they cannot find full-time work.

But some industries are prospering, like transportation and midpriced hotels. These have benefited from an enormous influx of tourists from the mainland after a liberalization by Beijing of exit visa rules for visits here.

Banking and other service industries are also thriving by tapping the mainland market.

Hong Kong's chief executive, Tung Chee-hwa, said in a speech on Monday that he thought that the territory could prosper by integrating its economy further with the mainland's. The economy here expanded at an annual rate of 6.8 percent in the first quarter, and growth in the second quarter, to be announced on Friday, is thought to have been even faster.

But Mr. Tung acknowledged that the years since the handover had been difficult.

"When we look back on the past seven years, it's hard to believe what we've been through: the bursting of the asset bubble, the collapse of the property market, years of deflation, the erosion of personal wealth, high unemployment, consumer pessimism, reduced public revenue and SARS," he said. "It was enough to cause anxiety in even the most confident of communities, and it certainly put a crimp in Hong Kong's style."

The modest inflation here in July was compared with even lower prices in the summer of 2003 at the end of an outbreak of severe acute respiratory syndrome. SARS devastated the city's economy as residents stayed home and tourists disappeared, prompting merchants to offer discounts and the government to offer a temporary reduction in utility rates.

Over the last six years, Hong Kong had become the symbol for economists warning of the dangers of deflation, as prices here swooned much more steeply even than in Japan.

The biggest effect of deflation was to destroy the savings of hundreds of thousands of Hong Kong families by lowering the value of many homes. At a time when soaring real estate values in the United States, Britain and other markets have captivated investors around the world, the fate of property owners in Hong Kong has been a chilling reminder that what goes up fast can come down hard.

While deflation caused food prices and wages to inch down, it caused property prices to plummet. Even after a substantial increase in the last year, offices still rent here for a little more than a third of what they did when Britain handed over the territory to China in 1997.

Homes sell for half what they did then, still an improvement from a year ago. According to the Hong Kong Monetary Authority, only 6 percent of homes are worth less than their mortgages now, compared with 22 percent a year ago.

A few deals this spring recalled the go-go days of the property bubble, like the $21.5 million sale of a 7,400-square-foot penthouse.

But such big-ticket transactions faded by late spring after Chinese stocks crashed in the wake of Beijing's decision to slow growth on the mainland to curb inflation.

Consumer prices on the mainland were 5.3 percent higher in July than a year earlier despite informal and formal government controls on the prices of many goods and services, while producer prices are climbing nearly twice as fast.

Despite years of deflation, Hong Kong is still not cheap. Last year, Hong Kong lost its ranking to Tokyo as the world's most expensive city for expatriates. But it still ranks fifth, behind Tokyo, London, Moscow and Osaka, Japan, according to an annual study by Mercer Human Resource Consulting.

The cost of living in Hong Kong remains 9.5 percent higher than in Manhattan, Mercer found.

The government did not release price statistics until after the close of trading on Monday afternoon. But Henry Tang, Hong Kong's financial secretary and third-ranking official, said Monday morning that he expected the figures to show an increase and herald a new direction for the territory's economy. The Hang Seng Index rose to 0.4 percent.

Along the same market where Mr. Sze sells thread, Lee Hsing-fat was waiting for customers late Monday afternoon in a small stall full of hardware, with rows of pliers, locks and chains on hooks. Chinese suppliers of pliers and glue have increased prices this year, with the glue producer raising prices by 5 percent recently with no warning, a rare step, he said.

"The products from other countries are the same price as before," Mr. Lee added.

Chan Kin Sun paused from selling fluorescent bulbs at a nearby stall and said that while he did not see a significant improvement in the economy, business conditions could be worse.

"The economy is a little bit better than last year," he said. "During SARS, it was very bad."

Growth Pace of Economy Slowed to 3.1% in 4th Quarter

By LOUIS UCHITELLE—January 29, 2005

THE American economy slowed to an annual growth rate of 3.1 percent in the final three months of 2004, the Commerce Department reported yesterday. That was the weakest quarterly pace in nearly two years, held down by a surge in imports, which substituted for production at home.

Consumers provided most of the lift, increasing their outlays for goods and services by more than enough to offset weaknesses in other areas. They spent most heavily on food and medical care, with home furnishings, home maintenance and motor vehicles not far behind.

"Spending was solid enough," said Edward McKelvey, a senior economist at Goldman Sachs, "but a lot of that spending was for imports. To me it says we are spending a lot and foreigners are continuing to eat our lunch."

The fourth-quarter performance of the gross domestic product was the worst of the year—nearly a percentage point below the 4 percent growth rate in the third quarter and the smallest rise since the first quarter of 2003.

But some forecasters predicted that economic growth would soon rebound, to an annual rate of at least 3.5 percent—mostly on the strength of consumer spending— and the Federal Reserve, in response, would continue its pattern of quarter-point increases in the federal funds rate. The funds rate influences the cost of mortgages, car loans and other consumer and business borrowing.

"We expect the Fed to tighten by a quarter of a point at each of the first four meetings of its policy makers this year," said Kenneth J. Matheny, a senior economist at Macroeconomic Advisers in St. Louis. With two more quarter-point increases in the second half, "we expect the funds rate to hit 3.75 percent by December," he said. The rate now is 2.25 percent.

Nigel Gault, an economist at Global Insight of Lexington, Mass, is not so sure. "The higher rates go," Mr. Gault said, "the more confident the Fed will have to be to keep on raising rates meeting after meeting. And this latest report is hardly stellar." By the measure used by most economists, gross domestic product, at nearly $11 trillion adjusted for inflation, was 3.7 percent higher in the fourth quarter than it was in the 2003 quarter.

That was not as good a performance as in the 12 months from the fourth quarter of 2002 to the fourth quarter of 2003. By another measure, however, one that takes average growth for 2004 and compares it with the average for 2003, last year's increase was 4.4 percent, the largest year-over-year rise since 1999.

The Bush administration focused on the more optimistic measure. "The addition of 2.3 million jobs and a solid year-over-year growth rate of 4.4 percent show the strength of the nation's economy," Treasury Secretary John W. Snow said yesterday.

Gross domestic product measures the value of all goods and services produced in the United States, including the value added in the marketing and retailing of imported products. The final number is calculated by adding together the value of all output, including the value of exported goods and services. From this number, the cost of imports is subtracted.

The surge in imports, mostly consumer products and petroleum, produced a large subtraction in the fourth quarter. A drop in exports, particularly in the export of machinery and other capital goods, made matters worse. The overall swing reduced the G.D.P. in the fourth quarter by 1.73 percentage points, the largest drop since the spring quarter of 1998.

"We are unlikely to get declines of this magnitude on a regular basis," Mr. Matheny said. The weakening dollar and growing prosperity abroad should raise the demand for American exports, he argued.

Until the fourth quarter, exports had risen for 15 consecutive months, although imports outpaced them and the trade deficit, as a result, has continued to grow. Some economists say the widening trade deficit could produce another quarter of weak economic growth this year, unless the dollar drops in value more than it has so far.

At the dollar's present level, "importers have largely absorbed the impact in the form of lower profit margins," Dean Baker, a director of the Center for Economic and Policy Research, wrote in his analysis of the latest G.D.P. numbers.

The strong consumer spending was for many economists the most encouraging news in yesterday's G.D.P. report. Personal consumption expenditures were up 4.6 percent, less than the third quarter's 5.1 percent rise, but ahead of increases in consumer spending in nearly every quarter over the last four years.

Relatively low interest rates and mild inflation as well as rising household wealth in the form of higher stock prices and home values all contributed to the strong consumer spending, economists said. So did an increase in personal disposable income, although Microsoft made a significant contribution to that increase with a one-time dividend paid to share-holders last year, according to yesterday's G.D.P. report.

Apart from consumer spending, noticeable contributions came from business investment and inventory accumulation. Wholesalers in particular increased their stockpiles of unsold merchandise, and business concentrated its spending on computers, software and other information-processing equipment.

"Basically I would characterize the investment numbers as strong in computers and software, but the outlays in other categories, including industrial equipment, mostly decelerated," said Brent Moulton, an associate director of the Commerce Department's Bureau of Economic Analysis, which produces the quarterly reports.

That trend, if it continues, puts pressure on consumers to keep the economy percolating, and Mr. Gault for one questions whether they can do this very much longer on the strength of their borrowing and the rising value of their homes and stock portfolios.

"At some point consumer spending has to come into line with income growth," he said, "and in 2004 income did not rise as fast as spending."

Brazil's President Is Cautious Despite Signs of a Recovery

By TODD BENSON—July 16, 2004

SÃO PAULO, Brazil, July 15—Exports are booming. Industrial production has risen for nine consecutive months. Retail sales are surging after a long slump. And unemployment is starting to retreat.

All these signs suggest that Brazil's economy, South America's largest, is rebounding more strongly than expected after taking its worst drubbing in more than a decade in 2003. The rosy economic indicators could not come at a better time for President Luiz Inácio Lula da Silva, a former lathe operator and union boss whose rise from poverty to the presidency in 2002 brought hope to millions of poor Brazilians.

On the campaign trail, Mr. da Silva, the leader of Brazil's Workers Party and a perennial presidential candidate, made lavish promises but was forced to enact an unpopular budget and monetary policies to stabilize Brazil's economy.

Now, after 18 months in office, the president is getting the results he needs to silence the increasingly vocal critics of his conservative economic policies.

Even so, Mr. da Silva is not claiming victory just yet. The president was widely criticized last year for boasting that a "growth spectacular" was right around the corner—only to watch the economy contract for the first time since 1992.

So when a recent batch of economic data showed that Brazilian industries were humming along at a lofty 82.5 percent of capacity, the most in 13 years, a humbled Mr. da Silva sounded a cautious note.

"I'm optimistic, but I'm also conscious that we have a lot of work to do before the economy really starts growing on a sustained basis," the president said on Monday during his weekly radio show. "We don't want an economy that grows one year and then backtracks the next. That's why we have to be cautious and we have to keep working with patience."

Patience is something that the left-leaning Mr. da Silva and his market-friendly team have been preaching tirelessly in recent months, and it finally appears they are getting their payoff. The tide began to shift in the government's favor in late May, when official data showed the economy expanding at a better-than-expected 2.7 percent in the first quarter from the period a year earlier. On an annualized basis, the growth rate for the quarter came in at 6.6 percent, far ahead of even the most optimistic forecasts.

Visibly relieved, government officials hailed the strong data as proof that the economy had turned the corner, prompting some analysts to raise their estimates for the year to about 4 percent from 3 percent to 3.5 percent. In 2003, Mr. da Silva's first year in office, the economy shrank 0.2 percent.

The first-quarter numbers also strengthened the hand of Mr. da Silva's finance minister, Antonio Palocci, who had become a magnet for criticism while the economy languished. Mr. Palocci, a one-time Trotskyite who has become a staunch defender of fiscal discipline, was thrust into the spotlight like a national hero, appearing on morning talk shows to assure Brazilians that good times were on the way.

"The impact those numbers had on diminishing the political pressure on the government was huge," said Marcelo Salomon, chief economist at Unibanco, Brazil's third-largest private sector bank. "Suddenly, all the talk about relaxing inflation targets as a way of speeding up the rebound was swatted down."

Still, critics claimed that the big-picture economic gains had yet to trickle down to the population and that the recovery was being driven almost exclusively by surging exports. Indeed, with unemployment hovering above 13 percent and real wages on the decline, most Brazilians had little reason to care that the economy was gaining steam.

But more recent data paints a different picture, suggesting that the rebound is spreading to other sectors of the economy. Industrial production soared 7.8 percent in May, buoyed by a jump in output in areas traditionally associated with domestic consumption, like shoes and leather products. Capital goods spending—a sign of investment—is on the rise, and consumers are finally flocking back to stores. Retail sales have risen for six consecutive months, jumping 10 percent in May. Car sales are also bouncing back, climbing 6.2 percent in June from May.

Retailers like Casas Bahia, a 372-store chain that sells big-ticket home fixtures from washing machines to furniture, were among the first to feel the recovery.

"About a month after Carnival it was clear that the economy was heating up," said Michael Klein, the company's finance director, referring to the pre-Lenten festival that fell in the last week of February this year. "But the recovery is widespread, it's not just us."

Citing the improved economic outlook, Casas Bahia, the country's largest retailer of household appliances, recently raised its sales forecast for the year to 8 billion reais (about $2.6 billion), from an initial estimate of 7 billion reais ($2.3 billion). In the first half of the year, the chain booked 3.6 billion reais ($1.2 billion) in sales, 20 percent more than expected.

"We're doing much better than we had anticipated," Mr. Klein said.

The jobs outlook also appears to be on the mend, albeit with less momentum than other economic indicators. Unemployment fell in May for the first time this year, dropping almost a full percentage point from the earlier month to 12.2 percent. And many economists say the jobless rate may be even lower since the government's statistics agency only surveys six major metropolitan areas. The data does not take into account rural areas, one of the fastest-growing job markets in Brazil because of a boom in agriculture.

"The missing link of the recovery had been on the jobs front," said Mário Mesquita, chief economist at ABN Amro in São Paulo, "but that's starting to change. Job creation is now beginning to catch up with the growth of the economically active population."

Brazil is not out of the woods yet. Inflation expectations have been on the rise for two months, meaning that the country's central bank has little room to significantly lower its benchmark interest rate—currently 16 percent—before the end of the year. Galloping oil prices and higher interest rates in the United States could add to infla-tionary pressure, further complicating the outlook.

More importantly, analysts say, Brazil needs to put in effect a host of policies to lure foreign investment and to set the stage for long-term growth. Mr. da Silva's government made some significant strides in this direction in 2003, overhauling the country's debt-ridden social security system and its byzantine tax system. But now the president is under pressure to clarify Brazil's ill-defined limits on foreign ownership, in particular to draw much-needed investment to the energy sector, and to modernize the country's bankruptcy and labor laws.

"There's enough fuel in the engine right now to get a meaningful rebound and then get a growth rate of about 3 percent," said Mohamed El-Erian, chief emerging markets portfolio manager at the Pacific Investment Management Company in Newport Beach, Calif. "But you're not looking at a takeoff to growth rates of about 6 percent. For that, you need a whole set of additional policies."

He added, "When growth wasn't materializing, it was difficult to get political support for these second-generation reforms. Fortunately, now it's getting to be a little bit easier."

Europe's Economy Hit Hard by Rapid Rise in Oil Prices

By MARK LANDLER—April 08, 2005

FRANKFURT, April 7—With oil trading well above $50 a barrel, the European Central Bank said Thursday that the high price was "very unwelcome," pulling down Europe's growth and pushing up inflation.

"We are now at a level that is very, very high," Jean-Claude Trichet, the bank's president, said at a news conference where he announced that the bank would not raise interest rates.

Europe's economy has shown signs of faltering in recent weeks, most visibly in surveys that report sharp drops in German industrial production and business confidence. On Monday, the European Commission cut its 2005 growth forecast for the 12-nation euro zone to 1.6 percent, from 2 percent.

The drumbeat of bad news has forced the European Central Bank to put off a long-signaled increase in its benchmark rate, which remains at 2 percent, a record low in the post-World War II period. In Britain, which is outside the European monetary union, the Bank of England also voted Thursday to leave its benchmark rate unchanged.

"Oil is by far the biggest threat to the world economy, and it is felt most by the weakest link, the European Union," said Thomas Mayer, the chief European economist at Deutsche Bank in London.

Mr. Mayer said high oil prices were most likely the main culprit for Germany's recent spate of bad numbers, including a surprising 2.2 percent decline in industrial production in February. Germany, as a major importer of oil, is particularly sensitive to spikes in the price.

Rising oil prices, however, also stoke inflation, which remains slightly above the 2 percent threshold set by the European Central Bank. The bank is laboring to balance its primary mission—serving as a sentinel against inflation—against its responsibility to foster economic growth.

Mr. Trichet made it clear that the bank still hoped to tighten monetary policy. A rate cut, which some economists advocate, is not an option, he said Thursday. But at the same time, he said the bank's governors did not discuss raising rates at their monthly policy meeting.

Sifting through the nuances of Mr. Trichet's pronouncements, most bank watchers now believe that a rate increase will not occur before the summer, and perhaps not until the end of the year.

"The bank's underlying message is the same, but his tone was somewhat less hawkish," said Jörg Krämer of the HVB Group in Munich.

He said he worried that the bank's unwillingness to budge—this is the 22nd month without a change in rates—was contributing to a bubble in property prices in some countries. Since 1998, he said, housing prices in Spain and France have risen more than in the United States.

Mr. Trichet described the economic data as mixed, saying it offered no evidence that Europe's fragile economy had gained any traction. He acknowledged that housing prices had risen sharply in a few countries.

Still, Mr. Trichet said the expansion of Europe's money supply and the loosening of credit was a cause for concern.

Political shadows now also loom over the European Central Bank and its common currency. In France, the faltering recovery and stubbornly high unemployment have swelled public opposition to the European Union's Constitution, which faces a referendum in late May.

Mr. Trichet, a Frenchman, said he believed that the Constitution would be approved. He urged doubters to recall the days before Europe adopted the euro, a period he said was one of chronic instability.

Economic Growth in China Is Stronger Than Expected

By KEITH BRADSHER—April 21, 2005

SHANGHAI, April 20—A soaring trade surplus and strong investment in new apartment buildings and office towers helped lift the Chinese economy to 9.5 percent growth in the first quarter, considerably stronger than expected and above the government's target of 8 percent, China's statistics agency announced on Wednesday.

The economy's heavy reliance on soaring exports and a feverish property market, in which luxury apartments change hands at steeply rising prices despite high vacancy rates, prompted concern among investors and economists alike.

Chinese stocks fell Wednesday on fears that Chinese authorities might feel compelled to raise interest rates to cool speculation in real estate. The Shanghai composite index dropped 1.31 percent and the Shenzhen composite index tumbled 1.83 percent.

Zheng Jingping, the spokesman of the National Bureau of Statistics, said that growth in investment in buildings and other fixed assets, at 22.8 percent in the first quarter compared with a year ago, was too high. "If the pace can be kept at about 20 percent, that will benefit the stable and healthy development of the Chinese economy," he said.

Investment growth was especially strong in urban real estate projects, at 26.7 percent in the first quarter. The People's Bank of China last month raised the down payment required in many cities for mortgages to 30 percent of the property's value, from 20 percent.

Wealth has become highly concentrated here, and growth in domestic demand has slowed somewhat for many goods as middle-class families economize. Sales dipped in the first quarter for all but the cheapest and the most expensive cars, for example.

But the luxury auto market remains strong. "Over all, the economy is still powering ahead," said Ian Robertson, the chairman and chief executive of Rolls-Royce, during a visit to the company's gleaming dealership here.

Rolls-Royce will hold the Asian introduction of its long-wheelbase Phantom here on Thursday. The car will retail in China at close to $800,000 because of steep Chinese taxes that double the price tag of luxury cars. China has become the company's fourth-largest market, narrowly trailing Japan, but still well behind the United States and Britain, Mr. Robertson said.

Part of the demand comes from entrepreneurs who have grown wealthy in the property market. Several construction cranes stood across the street from the Rolls-Royce dealership, and Mr. Robertson pointed to them, calling them the "national symbols of China."

A spurt in exports, which jumped 35 percent and led to a near-record surplus of $16.6 billion for the quarter, also stepped up pressure on China to allow its currency, known as the yuan or renminbi, to appreciate against the United States dollar and other currencies.

A stronger yuan would make Chinese exports more expensive and less competitive in foreign markets, and would make it easier for foreign companies to increase sales here. Chinese imports have stagnated except for raw materials, especially oil from the Middle East and Africa. The Bush administration in particular, and European and Japanese officials to a lesser extent, have been calling for China to let the yuan rise, most recently when finance ministers in the Group of 7 nations met in Washington last weekend.

James J. Padilla, the president and chief operating officer of the Ford Motor Company, issued a thinly veiled warning here late Wednesday that American manufacturers would not tolerate high trade deficits in the United States indefinitely.

"How long will the U.S. be an open market where imports just come in? It won't be forever," he said at a dinner with reporters in Shanghai that was part of preparations for the public opening of the Shanghai Auto Show this weekend.

Ford and especially General Motors have been losing market share steadily for many years, mainly to Japanese automakers, though Mr. Padilla warned that Chinese automakers would eventually start trying to enter the American market. "That will develop over time, but it's not tomorrow," he said.

Several investment banks, notably J. P. Morgan, have been predicting that a change in Chinese currency policy could come soon, either in the coming weeks or on July 1, given Chinese officialdom's penchant for making important economic decisions at the middle or end of the year. But the sometimes violent street protests against Japan may have delayed any move by creating an atmosphere of political uncertainty that may discourage the government from taking any potentially risky economic moves.

Several senior Chinese officials expressed strong reservations last month about any change in the value of the currency.

One benefit of allowing currency appreciation is that it would make it cheaper for Chinese companies to buy oil and other commodities that are priced in dollars. The consumer price index here was 2.8 percent higher in the first quarter than a year ago, well below the level of 4 percent to 5 percent that the government has said would be a problem. But producer prices, which tend to be less regulated, have been rising twice as fast.

"Although we think the C.P.I. rise in the first quarter was quite mild, we can't be complacent and we need to seriously increase monitoring," Mr. Zheng said.

At the Canton Trade Fair last Friday in Guangzhou, China, many managers were complaining about the high cost of oil, which is driving up the cost of plastic, polyester and other materials. Wang Zhi Gang, a manager of the Yantai Tiancheng Textiles Import and Export Corporation in Yantai, China, said,

"We have to ask our customers to pay more," he said.

Chris Buckley in Beijing contributed reporting for this article.

Boom Time's Inflation Proves Stubborn in Ireland

By BRIAN LAVERY—November 16, 2004

DUBLIN, Nov. 15—Most people in Ireland realized it a while ago, and the government has finally acknowledged it: along with insufferable traffic jams and longer working hours, the Celtic Tiger boom of the 1990's left Ireland saddled with some of the highest prices in Europe.

Inflation began climbing in 1998 and reached a peak of 7 percent in 2000, as the economy experienced double-digit growth. But now, officials in the Department of Finance proudly point to figures like those published last week, showing that inflation has fallen to a respectable 2.5 percent in the last year.

But a recent report by a government-run research organization, the National Competitiveness Council—in one of its rare statements on a specific economic issue—found that Ireland was practically tied with Finland as the most expensive country in the euro currency zone, and that only Denmark, which does not use the euro, is more expensive.

The change has been across the board, from groceries and clothing to services and utilities, and the price increases have caused a gradual series of social, as well as economic, effects.

Housing prices are still rising quickly—up 14 percent in 2003, according to the Irish mortgage lender Irish Life and Permanent. Those high prices prevent young people from settling down in their own cities or cripple them with huge amounts of debt. By September, the rate of growth in housing prices had moderated slightly. But houses still averaged 252,431 euros ($324,636) nationwide and 330,603 euros ($425,169) in Dublin.

Young couples furnishing new homes fly to Scotland on Ryanair, the low-budget airline, to shop at Ikea, because zoning laws prevent the company from opening its furniture warehouses in Ireland. In a weekly column, The Irish Times compares the prices of everyday goods, like microwave meals and electric toothbrushes, which range from 12.25 to 21.50 euros ($15.54 to $27.27). Travel agents say they book hundreds of Christmas shoppers each weekend on trips to New York.

And consumers can be heard complaining about prices just about everywhere.

"You're spending 60 euros, where you used to spend 50 for the same amount of stuff," said Brian Payne, a 40-year-old bookkeeper carrying two bags of groceries outside a Tesco supermarket in a central Dublin shopping mall. When he bought a television recently, Mr. Payne said, he sought out a discount electronics outlet because regular stores were too expensive, and then bought a generic model. "I used to be able to get the name brand," he said.

And now that a pint of Guinness stout costs $5, and lagers like Heineken or Budweiser cost nearly $6, the Irish go out a lot less, and keg sales have fallen more than 5 percent in the last year, according to the Irish Brewers' Association. From 2000 to last year, the price of a pint rose 20 percent, or 70 cents, and has edged up further since.

Beamish stout, Guinness's bitter rival, increased its sales by 140,000 pints last quarter when it promised to delay a price increase until next year, said Ruth Norton, marketing manager.

The tourism industry, long a mainstay of the Irish economy, saw the warning signs first, because of feedback from international visitors, and the government cabinet minister for tourism has issued several stern warnings to hotels and restaurants that they would eventually price themselves out of the market. In a survey last year, 13 percent of visiting North Americans told the state agency Tourism Ireland that they were dissatisfied with "value for money" on an Irish vacation, up from 4 percent in 2001.

"Consumers are definitely reacting," said Jim Power, chief economist of Friends First Asset Management in Dublin. Growth in retail sales, which was 11 percent in 2001, tapered to around 2 percent this year, he said.

Most analysts said that Ireland's period of runaway inflation was a result of some short-sighted government spending and some inevitable fiscal changes at the introduction of the euro, like rapid exchange rate fluctuations and ceding control of interest rates to the European Central Bank. But the analysts do not see high prices today as a problem.

Inflation is a "natural element" of Ireland's rapid economic growth, said Austin Hughes, an economist at IIB Bank, a mortgage lender with more than $9 billion in assets. "It's a consequence rather than a leading indicator," he said. And given the benefits of Ireland's economic growth in the last decade, "it's probably a cost that we're willing to pay."

Businesses are also feeling the impact: energy costs are up more than 20 percent since 2000, and rents for retailers have almost doubled. But companies in the service sector keep margins high by passing price increases on to customers, said David Croughan, chief economist at the Irish Business and Employers' Confederation, an employers' lobby group.

Manufacturers, which are more affected by international competition, lack the ability to pass on rising costs, and prices for their goods have recently declined to about the levels they were in 1999. But manufacturers are still enjoying an overall drop in labor costs because of productivity increases from long before the boom began, and to recent downsizing. Ireland was "almost super-competitive" in 1999 when the euro currency came into effect, Mr. Croughan said.

Ireland remains at nearly full employment, and wages have kept pace—rising 37.1 percent before tax from 1998 to 2003, and 12.1 percent in real terms that account for inflation. So, basic necessities have not been put out of reach. The Competitiveness Council survey found that gross average pay is now 38,140 euros ($48,370) in Ireland, compared with 35,750 euros ($45,339) in Britain and 40,470 euros ($51,325) in the United States.

That has not stopped people from feeling cheated when they see price tags creeping upward every month. "You have to work to a budget now," said Karen Reilly, 23, a trainee beautician, while buying clothes for her children in shops already glittering with Christmas decorations. She was conscious of spending more on household bills as well as retail purchases.

Mr. Payne, the bookkeeper, said that he was considering moving to another country because prices, particularly for houses, are high enough to make him more skeptical about life here. "I used to be the kind of person who loved Ireland," he said.

Zimbabwe, Long Destitute, Teeters Toward Ruin

By MICHAEL WINES—May 21, 2005

BULAWAYO, Zimbabwe—In the weeks before parliamentary elections in March, the leaders of this threadbare nation threw open the national larder, wooing voters with stocks of normally scarce gasoline and corn and a flood of freshly printed money.

It may have helped: the ruling party, President Robert G. Mugabe's ZANU-PF, was installed for another five years. But Zimbabwe's Potemkin prosperity has evaporated since the elections, replaced by penury and mounting signs of economic collapse.

Here in the second largest city, lines of cars stretch a quarter mile and more at fuel-parched service stations, and drivers spend the night in their cars' back seats lest they lose their place in line. Milk, cooking oil and, most of all, corn, the national staple, are a distant memory at most stores. At one downtown grocery, tubes of much-prized American toothpaste are kept in a locked case.

Zimbabwe's currency, which traded on the black market at 120 to the dollar in April 2002, went for 6,200 to the dollar last December, 12,000 on April 1, and 17,000 in early May. By mid-May a single American dollar brought as much as 25,000 Zimbabwean dollars, though the rate has since steadied at about 20,000.

Zimbabwe's government steadfastly maintained an official exchange rate of about 6,100 Zimbabwean dollars per American dollar until Thursday, when the nation's reserve bank announced a devaluation. But business managers here say the new official rate—9,000 per American dollar—is unlikely to have more than a brief impact on the economy.

"It's running out of control," one Bulawayo manufacturer said in an interview. "When you're going down a path of destruction, you can keep putting patches on the tires—patch, patch, patch—but eventually the tire is going to burst."

Business executives interviewed for this article almost uniformly refused to be named, fearing that criticism of economic policies would doom their scant chances of receiving government assistance.

One persistent critic, John Robertson, a former government economist, said the government appeared to have exhausted its reserves on the feel-good campaign before the parliamentary elections and was now paying the price.

For years, of course, Zimbabwe's economy has been a chewing-gum and baling-wire affair, with 70 percent unemployment, triple-digit inflation and a currency no foreign creditor will accept. Prosperity has been receding since the late 1990's, when the government's attacks on international creditors and its seizure of commercial farms set off a cascade of economic backlashes.

Past economic plunges have provoked food riots, gas-line protests and government crackdowns. This time the government has sent the police to quell mobs outside groceries and gas stations, and started rounding up street merchants who deal too openly in black-market goods and selling currency at illicit rates.

Yet some say that the current crisis, perhaps the worst since the economy began foundering, may mark a turning point. Zimbabwe's main economic problems—capital flight, a dire shortage of foreign exchange with which to buy imports, and turbocharged inflation—are now so severe that they are eroding what remains of the industrial and agricultural base.

Manufacturing has slowed to a trickle, hamstrung by shortages of fuel and imported components. Businesses have been driven to barter and the black market, adding to the inflation. Appeals for government help are mostly fruitless. The government is all but broke.

"The scarcities now are coming from manufacturers who can't deliver enough to retailers to fill their shelves," Mr. Robertson said in an interview in Harare, the capital.

Initially the problem was that manufacturers could not cobble together enough supplies to make their products. "Now that there are more critical shortages in things like fuel," he said, "it's almost academic whether they can get the material, because they can't deliver the products anyway. The end result of the shortages is that prices are rising."

In Harare in the second week of May, rumors that a shipment of sugar had arrived created a line half a mile long outside one suburban supermarket. Yet the problem, Mr. Robertson said, was not so much a shortage of sugar as a shortage of the imported polyethylene bags that hold it.

Coca-Cola is being rationed because the gas used for carbonation is in short supply and the local bottler cannot find foreign currency to buy the imported syrup. Virtually any product made of steel is hard to find, because most rolled steel is imported from South Africa, and South African steel mills are demanding cash up front from Zimbabwean customers.

"It's what I call a chain-link economy," said one Bulawayo maker of a basic steel commodity. "Company A manufactures parts for Company B, and Company B manufactures a part for Company C, and so on until company F makes the finished product. What's happening is that the links are falling apart."

That manufacturer offers a line of 25 products. Only four are being made, because he cannot find paint, abrasives and braces to make the others. "They're all imported," he said of the materials, "and if there's no foreign currency, then my supplier can't buy them to sell to me."

Zimbabwe's immediate problem is that it has run out of foreign currency. But that is only one domino in a long chain that threatens to bury the economy.

Agricultural exports were an economic mainstay. But in the last five years, Zimbabwe's parceling out of 5,000 commercial farms among squatters and peasants has caused the collapse of commercial farming. That has destroyed the businesses that supported it, from tractor sales—the nation needs 50,000, and has fewer than 400 working ones—to irrigation suppliers.

That only deepened the export tailspin: Zimbabwean tobacco production is down two-thirds in five years, for instance, and the quality, once world renowned, is so poor that buyers are scarce.

Falling exports made foreign currency more expensive, causing exchange rates to rocket. But the government has generally chosen to print more money instead of readjusting the value of its currency; Zimbabwe's money supply rose 226 percent in 2004.

The result has been hyperinflation and a thriving black market in money and goods. Hyperinflation and the artificial exchange rate, in turn, have crippled gold mining, Zimbabwe's other big export industry. Production fell 18 percent in the first quarter of 2005.

The government's latest devaluation of the Zimbabwe dollar sets special, higher exchange rates for exports of gold and cotton, two major industries facing collapse in the current crisis. The loss of either would crimp foreign-currency receipts even more; a collapse in cotton would pull Zimbabwe's textile industry down as well.

The higher exchange rates effectively are subsidies, costing the government the equivalent of scores of millions of American dollars. Asked how the government would get the money to subsidize the two industries, the economist, Mr. Robertson, said, "My feeling is that they'll print it."

The government said Friday that it would also budget more money to import grain, hoping to avert what some experts say is a looming famine when the harvest that ends in May—by all accounts a dismal failure—has been consumed.

Zimbabwe needs about 1.6 million tons of grain a year, and officials say they intend to purchase 1.2 million tons. But corn imports from South Africa, Zimbabwe's only supplier of note, totaled a bare 37,500 tons in the last month, far short of demand. It is unclear where the government will find the foreign currency it needs to buy grain abroad.

Starved for foreign currency to import crucial supplies, the government now requires all businesses to trade 25 percent of their foreign income at the official exchange rate. That hits businesses with a double whammy: they have less foreign money to buy imported raw materials, and they must raise prices to make up their currency losses.

If that seems a formula for more shortages and more inflation, few business managers here would disagree.

Tony Rowland, the chief executive of Bulawayo-based Zimplow, employs 400 people to make animaldrawn plows from steel rolled at one of Zimbabwe's few domestic mills. To hedge against the constantly rising price of domestic steel, he reinvests his profits in something that rises with inflation: nuts and bolts.

"I've become a steel dealer," he said. "I've had to expand my business to things beyond my core business to keep going." Were he forced to buy and sell at the official exchange rate, he said, "I'd be dead in the water."

Mr. Rowland and others say that even partial devaluations of the currency by the government will not revive the economy or save businesses and that an economic overhaul that reflected reality would impose unacceptable suffering on ordinary citizens who already undergo too many hardships.

"Something's got to give," said another Bulawayo manufacturer, a major exporter. "The problem is that the decisions to be made are so radical, and would affect the average man so badly, that they'll never be made. Not under the current environment, anyway."

So Zimbabweans muddle through. In Harare, the chief of a major consumer products company said recently that he had junked his accounting software until programmers could adapt a Turkish version to his requirements. The problem: the Zimbabwe spreadsheets cannot accommodate the flood of zeros required for transactions that now run into the billions—even the trillions—of Zimbabwean dollars.

"We've run out of noughts," he said.

Higher Gas Prices Cut Consumer Spending

By JENNIFER BAYOT—April 14, 2005

CONSUMERS spent more on gasoline last month and far less than expected over all, the government said yesterday, suggesting that prices at the pump are starting to curb other purchases.

The Commerce Department reported that retail sales in March rose 0.3 percent, to $339 billion, a slower rate than the 0.5 percent increase in February and significantly below Wall Street's forecasts for an increase of 0.8 percent, according to Bloomberg News.

"Higher gasoline prices had an impact on discretionary spending, and obviously a more powerful impact than forecasters thought they were going to have," said David Greenlaw, an economist with Morgan Stanley.

The new numbers and other recent data, including a slowdown in job growth and a widening trade deficit, suggest that the economy is expanding at a more tepid pace, which could ease the Federal Reserve's concerns about inflation.

Consumers, encouraged by incentives, pushed auto sales up 0.7 percent, the Commerce Department said. Excluding the volatile auto sector, retail sales rose only 0.1 percent.

With higher oil prices, gas stations drew nearly 0.9 percent of consumers' spending at $29.6 billion, a 2.1 percent jump.

To get a better picture of discretionary spending, economists often exclude spending at auto dealerships and gas stations. In that case, retail sales fell 0.1 percent, the first such decline since April 2004.

"This was a downer," said Robert J. Barbera, chief economist at ITG/Hoenig, a brokerage firm in Rye Brook, N.Y. Added to other economic data, the figures suggest that "the notion that the economy was really taking off and really firing on all cylinders is wrong."

The numbers show an unexpected weakening in consumer spending, which amounts to two-thirds of total economic activity.

Behind that growth were the lowest interest rates on consumer debt since the 1960's, but the specter of rising rates may be joining higher energy costs and slower wage growth in damping shoppers' spirits.

Cold weather in March may have been partly to blame, economists said, keeping people home and making spring fashions unappealing. Sales at specialty clothing stores dropped 1.2 percent. Sales at department stores fell 0.7 percent.

Long on Cash,
Short on Ideas

By ANNA BERNASEK—December 05, 2004

MONEY affects people in different ways—it emboldens some but makes others cautious. Right now, healthy profits seem to have made corporate leaders meek. Business investment seems to be losing steam. And growth in jobs and the overall economy could soon sputter, too.

What's holding companies back? Can anything be done to rev up their investment spending?

After the 2001 recession, economists looked in vain for an expected rebound in spending by companies. The long-awaited recovery showed up in the second half of 2003, but it has slowed sharply in the third quarter of this year.

According to recent government figures, gross private investment grew at a mere 3 percent annual rate in the third quarter after expanding at a double-digit pace for the previous four quarters. The upshot is that corporate America's contribution to overall growth was cut by two-thirds during the last quarter, to 12 percent from an average of 40 percent in the previous four quarters.

There's no mystery about what has changed. The main force behind the investment recovery—spending on technology—grew at a 13 percent pace in the second quarter, then just 7 percent in the third quarter.

"I think capital spending has done its thing for this recovery," said Nariman Behravesh, chief economist at Global Insight, an economic forecasting firm. "While I don't expect it to fall out of bed, it will slow down."

Mr. Behravesh is in good company. Most economists are forecasting weaker business spending next year.

But hang on. It's not supposed to be like this. By this point in the economic cycle, strong profits would be expected to translate into pretty spectacular investment spending, spurring dynamic growth in jobs and in the overall economy. Ideally, that should create a self-sustaining cycle of ever higher profits, investment and economic growth.

But instead of investing, corporate America has been accumulating cash—big piles of it. According to the most recent figures from the Federal Reserve Board, nonfinancial corporations increased their liquid assets by 20 percent, to a record $1.3 trillion, from the start of 2003 to June 2004.

Think about all that money for a minute. It's about 10 percent of the total economy, and much of it is virtually stuffed into a mattress.

It's not the normal state of affairs. In a recent speech, a Fed governor, Roger W. Ferguson Jr., highlighted the unusual trend. Historically, capital spending has almost always been larger than a company's cash flow, according to Mr. Ferguson. That is because corporate leaders usually have a lot more ideas about how to generate future profits than they have cash on hand to do it. Today, it's the opposite. Companies seem to have more cash than ideas.

So what's going on in all those thick-carpeted boardrooms? Have managers really run out of good ideas? One can only speculate. Mr. Ferguson said the cash buildup was a troubling sign of weak confidence.

"Given the current low interest rates, the preference for holding financial assets over expanding operations suggests that businesses lack confidence in the future profitability of their potential ventures," he said. Factors like high oil prices, international tension, immense budget deficits, high consumer debt and stretched consumer budgets could be weighing on decision makers.

But there are other considerations. Consider all the investment opportunities out there. Is it possible that corporate leaders just can't find enough acceptable opportunities to expand their operations—at least not at home? Or perhaps it's a question of expectations. Executives who became accustomed to rich returns during the bubble years may not have adjusted their expectations to the current climate. They could be holding on, waiting for the home run that seems never to happen.

Whatever the reason for holding back, there remains a huge untapped potential for the economy. But that potential may never be fully realized. Investors recognize the problem, which is sometimes called the bladder principle. Uncomfortably large cash reserves build pressure for managers to spend. At a certain point, they may seek relief without due consideration of the wisdom of their spending.

Ultimately, the fear of wasting hard-earned dollars leads companies to sit on their hands or, as Microsoft chose so dramatically, to return the hoard to shareholders rather than invest it.

With so much potential sitting idle, can anything be done to encourage wise business investment? One popular recent approach has been to allow businesses to accelerate the depreciation of their investments, a tax incentive that encouraged buying of certain items. Legislation allowing this went into effect in 2002 and will expire at the end of this year. But so far, evidence suggests that the policy's economic impact has been modest.

Two economists at the University of Michigan, Christopher L. House and Matthew D. Shapiro, recently studied the policy and found that while the accelerated depreciation rates did bolster spending on long-life assets, the effect on the overall economy was not large.

THEY calculated that the policy might have increased output by 0.1 percent over all and resulted in 100,000 more jobs. As the policy expires at the end of this year, those gains could shrink. In any case, government incentives have their limits. "A firm isn't going to want to install capital, even if it's cheap, if it can't use it in the future," Professor Shapiro said. "If people come to expect we'll have a relatively strong economy over the next few years, that will be more important than any of these tax changes."

That insight may be crucial to understanding the problem.

The best path forward may not be paved with a clever government fix but rather with a steady diet of fiscal responsibility, wise international diplomacy and price stability. And for individual businesses, the task may be refocusing on the difficult and expensive path of investing steadily and courageously in their long-term strategies.

Subtracting a bit from those cash piles could add nicely to the economy.

Fears Mount That Germany Faces Recession

By MARK LANDLER—April 27, 2005

FRANKFURT, April 26—Six influential German economic institutes have cut their growth forecast for this year in half, prompting a new rash of fears that the German economy is on the brink of recession.

After four years of lackluster growth, the downward revision—to 0.7 percent from 1.5 percent—illustrates that economic forecasting in Germany has become mostly an exercise in finding ever-more-precise ways to measure stagnation, economists say.

In their semiannual report on the German economy, submitted Tuesday, the six institutes said: "Almost no other country in the European Union has had a development in recent years that was so unfavorable. Obviously, the German economy is suffering from fundamental weakness."

Given such weak underpinnings, economists said it was quite possible that the German economy, Europe's largest and an engine for much of the Continent, could fall into a recession—classically defined as two consecutive quarters of contraction.

But this, they said, would scarcely be different from the current state of affairs.

"Trend growth in Germany is now so low that you can easily meet the technical definition of recession," said Thomas Mayer, the chief European economist at Deutsche Bank in London.

In fact, Mr. Mayer said, he viewed the forecast as optimistic because it assumes that Germany will keep growing, despite the spike in oil prices and the softening of the global economy.

"If oil prices keep going up, Germany won't even hold on to the 0.7 percent number," he said. "You would end up with stagnation, and more importantly, there would be no recovery next year."

Even without rising oil prices, there is no shortage of grim news in the report. The institutes, which generally anticipate the government's own forecast, predict that growth will be only 1.5 percent in 2006, less than in 2004, which was 1.6 percent.

With a growth rate this anemic, economists say, Germany cannot generate new jobs.

The current unemployment rate of 12 percent is a record in the post-World War II period, and poses a mounting political threat to Chancellor Gerhard Schröder. He faces a difficult state election next month in North Rhine-Westphalia, Germany's depleted industrial heartland.

"We had hoped that domestic growth would pick up, but there is no sign of that happening," said Bert Rürup, the head of Mr. Schröder's council of economic advisers.

Germany needs to grow from 1.5 percent to 2 percent a year, Mr. Rürup said, to generate significant new jobs.

While it has been able to increase exports, even with the handicap of a strong euro, it has not found a way to encourage consumer spending, a critical factor for reviving its moribund domestic economy.

"Germany has no short-term competitiveness problem," Mr. Rürup said. "It has a long-term growth problem."

Some private economists take a more positive view.

Consumer confidence, they note, rose slightly in a recent survey by the GfK Group, a market research firm in Nuremberg. And the damping effects of the euro may have passed.

Jörg Krämer , the chief economist at the HVB Group in Munich, said that if oil prices remained steady, growth in Germany should bounce back in the second half of 2005.

This, he admits, is a big if. The Ifo Institute in Munich, one of the six institutes that lowered the growth forecast, released a separate business survey on Monday showing the third consecutive monthly decline in corporate confidence in April.

Oil prices, economists say, are the main culprit for this, since Germany is one of the world's leading importers.

The effect of high oil prices is being felt throughout Europe, and is one reason the European Central Bank has been reluctant to start raising interest rates, despite its stated desire to do so.

On Tuesday, the bank's vice president, Lucas Papademos, said there was little evidence that growth was picking up in the 12-nation euro zone. His comments suggest no imminent change in the bank's monetary policy.

Indeed, some economists say rates could remain as they are until 2006. The German government, meanwhile, seems at a loss for a quick fix. It has begun to overhaul the labor market, through a package of measures known as the Hartz reforms.

Mr. Rürup said that if Germany had a more flexible labor market, it could create jobs with a lower growth rate.

Critics say these measures, while helpful, are only a half step. They make it easier for employers to hire temporary workers and create entry-level jobs for people who have been out of work. But they do not attack the job-protection rules that make it hard to lay off workers.

"They need to face down the unions," Mr. Mayer at Deutsche Bank said. "But they won't— neither the government nor the opposition."

Deficits and Tax System Changes in Bush's Second-Term Economy

By EDMUND L. ANDREWS—November 04, 2004

WASHINGTON, Nov. 3—Even as President Bush was celebrating his election victory on Wednesday, his Treasury Department provided an ominous reminder about the economic challenges ahead.

After four years of rapidly rising budget deficits, the Treasury announced on Wednesday morning that the government will borrow $147 billion in the first three months of 2005—a new quarterly record, but one that is likely to be eclipsed before that year is out.

Empowered by his own victory and stronger Republican majorities in Congress, Mr. Bush has pledged to push an economic agenda that could be more ambitious than the $1.9 trillion worth of tax cuts over 10 years that he signed in his first term.

The new economic agenda will focus on two big goals. One is expected to aim for a fundamental overhaul of the income tax, very likely in the direction of a system that lessens even further the taxation of investment income; the other to push for a partial privatization of Social Security that could eventually reduce costs but require borrowing more than $2 trillion over the next two decades.

The challenge ahead can be seen in the fiscal decline that took place between Mr. Bush's first inauguration in 2001 and his second one on Jan. 20, 2005. Federal tax revenue was $100 billion lower this year than when Mr. Bush took office, but spending is $400 billion higher.

The ballooning budget deficits, which could total $5 trillion over the next 10 years if Mr. Bush succeeds in making his tax cuts permanent, could constrain the president's choices far more than they have in the first term.

Foreign investors have thus far been willing to finance the United States' borrowing, but most of that has come from central banks of Asian nations rather than private investors. If foreign appetite for Treasury securities wanes, interest rates would have to rise to make such investments attractive enough to keep money flowing into this country.

"The U.S. bond markets are likely to react very badly," said Nariman Behravesh, chief economist at Global Insight, an economic forecasting company, "as investors begin to worry about the impact of these large deficits on U.S. interest rates, the U.S. current account deficit and the dollar."

Making the job more difficult, politically as well as economically, is that higher oil prices have slowed American growth even as job creation continues to languish. Consumer and business confidence have slipped markedly in the last few months. And while oil prices declined modestly over several days until a $1.26-a-barrel rise on Wednesday, most forecasters are expecting economic growth to slow to 3 percent in 2005 from about 4 percent this year.

Slower growth would aggravate Mr. Bush's budget problems. The war in Iraq and the continued occupation of Afghanistan could exceed $100 billion next year, according to a Republican analyst. None of that has been included in an administration plan for reducing the budget deficit by half over five years.

Mr. Bush has also promised to make his tax cuts permanent, which would add nearly $1 trillion to federal debt by 2014. And to avoid a huge tax increase for the upper middle class, he hopes to re-engineer the alternative minimum tax, a parallel tax that was created to prevent wealthy people from overusing tax deductions but that is expected to engulf as many as 30 million families by the end of this decade. That could cost more than $500 billion.

The biggest problem of all is the one that begins at the end of this decade: the looming retirement of 76 million baby boomers, which is expected to add trillions of dollars in new costs for Social Security and Medicare benefits.

Budget analysts say Mr. Bush can no longer blame slower economic growth or a weak stock market for the budget deficit, as he has in much of his first term, and he cannot count on faster economic growth to close the gap over the next four years.

"Policy choices will determine where we go," said Douglas Holtz-Eakin, director of the nonpartisan Congressional Budget Office. "We will not grow our way out of this. It is no longer the case that we can blame everything on the economy."

During his first term, President Bush never vetoed a spending bill, including measures that greatly increased farm subsidies and added more than $140 billion in new corporate tax breaks. But even though Republicans have now expanded their control over both houses of Congress, Mr. Bush is likely to face bruising new conflicts as soon as lawmakers return for a lame-duck session to pass spending bills for the coming year.

He has threatened to veto a three-year bill for highways and mass transportation, which would spend tens of billions more than he wants. Meanwhile, to save money, Republican lawmakers have pared back a number of Mr. Bush's proposals for higher spending on favored programs like space exploration and foreign development assistance.

Mr. Bush could face his first test this month, when Congress tries to pass spending bills covering most areas outside the military and homeland security. The Senate proposals would run $8 billion higher than the House bills, and they include some of Mr. Bush's priorities in education.

William Gale and Peter Orszag, budget analysts at the Brookings Institution, estimated that budget deficits would remain at today's levels—equivalent to roughly 3.5 percent of the gross domestic product—for the next 10 years if Mr. Bush's tax cuts are extended and if Congress extends other tax cuts that have generally been renewed in the past.

And that does not count the $500 billion for repairing the alternative minimum tax. Mr. Bush ordered the Treasury to come up with a comprehensive solution by early next year, and that proposal could form the basis of a broader plan to overhaul the income-tax system. Even if the costs of repairing the tax are submerged in a larger plan, they will be difficult to avoid.

More ominiously, said Mr. Holtz-Eakin, who worked in the Bush White House before becoming head of the Congressional Budget Office, there is little room for error. Almost any unexpected shock—a new recession, or a new military crisis—could push budget shortages higher than the gloomiest forecasters are predicting now.

And even if Washington gets through the current uncertainties, only four years remain until the oldest baby boomers start to retire and the costs of Social Security and Medicare benefits gradually eclipse those of every other part of the federal government.

Greenspan Says Federal Budget Deficits Are 'Unsustainable'

By EDMUND L. ANDREWS—March 03, 2005

WASHINGTON, March 2—Alan Greenspan, chairman of the Federal Reserve, warned on Wednesday that the federal budget deficits were "unsustainable," and he urged Congress to scrutinize both spending and taxes to solve the problem.

Mr. Greenspan also warned that the deficits could be driven sharply higher by costs connected to the aging of the baby boom generation, particularly entitlement programs like Social Security and Medicare. While reiterating his support for President Bush's plan to offer private accounts as part of over-hauling Social Security, Mr. Greenspan urged lawmakers to tackle the program's problems now, rather than later.

The assessment was Mr. Greenspan's gloomiest to date about the government's budget straits. Unless Congress takes major action to reduce the deficits, preferably, he said, by deep cuts in spending, annual budgetary short-falls will continue and closing those gaps will become even more difficult.

Though Mr. Greenspan has made similar pleas in the past, he spoke more urgently on Wednesday and disagreed more adamantly with Republican lawmakers and Mr. Bush, who have steadfastly refused to put restrictions on new tax cuts.

"Addressing the government's own imbalances will require scrutiny of both spending and taxes," Mr. Greenspan told members of the House Budget Committee. "However, tax increases of sufficient dimension to deal with our looming fiscal problems arguably pose signifi-cant risks to economic growth and the revenue base."

The Fed chairman emphasized that his own preference was to reduce deficits by cutting spending rather than raising taxes. But he said the "overriding principle" was to reduce the deficit, making compromise essential.

"It's the principle that I think is involved here, namely that you cannot continuously introduce legislation which tends to expand the budget deficit," Mr. Greenspan said.

The Fed chairman's tone, as he addressed the House Budget Committee on Wednesday, was noticeably more urgent than it was last year or even in Congressional hearings just a few weeks ago.

"When you begin to do the arith-metic of what the rising debt level implied by the deficits tells you, and you add interest costs to that ever-rising debt, at ever-higher interest rates, the system becomes fiscally destabilizing," he told lawmakers. "Unless we do some-thing to ameliorate it in a very significant manner," he added, "we will be in a state of stagnation."

White House officials played down Mr. Greenspan's remarks, noting that he had placed top priority on reduced government spending and that Mr. Bush had vowed to reduce the budget deficit by half by 2009.

"The president does have a substantial deficit-reduction package," said Trent Duffy, a White House spokesman. "His budget is a continuation of that policy, and he looks forward to working with Congress in cutting that spending down. Likewise, the president agrees that the long-term budget is the issue, which is why he's trying to lead a national discussion and reform movement to save and strengthen Social Security."

Mr. Greenspan's comments deepened a long-running disagree-ment between the Federal Reserve and the White House, and they come at a moment when House and Senate leaders are trying to hammer out a budget resolution or blueprint for tax and spending bills this year.

Mr. Greenspan, a Republican, has long argued that Congress should reinstate rules that would require lawmakers to offset the cost of tax cuts and new spending programs with savings in other areas.

Mr. Bush and his Republican allies in Congress have insisted that any such "pay as you go" restric-tions, which existed in the 1990's, apply only to new spending and not to new tax cuts.

Reinstating the previous budget rules would make it far more difficult, if not almost impossible, for Congress to extend permanently Mr. Bush's tax cuts of 2001 and 2003.

Extending all of the expiring tax cuts add about $1.8 trillion to the federal debt over 10 years, according to the Congressional Budget Office. That would come on top of a rapid escalation in the federal debt from $3.4 trillion to $4.3 trillion as a result of soaring annual deficits since 2001.

House and Senate lawmakers are hoping to unveil a budget resolution as early as next week, and many Republicans want to include provisions that would allow the Senate to approve tax cuts this year with a simple majority of 51 votes. Without a budget resolution, Senate rules effectively require that such tax cuts be approved by a two-thirds majority.

None of Mr. Bush's big tax cuts are scheduled to expire this year, but the 2003 tax cuts on stock dividends and capital gains are to expire in 2008, and the other big tax cuts are all to expire by the end of 2011.

Making all of those tax cuts permanent, as Mr. Bush wants, would add about $1.8 trillion to the federal debt over 10 years, the nonpartisan Congressional Budget Office says.

In addition to calling for a return to the tough budget rules of the 1990's, the last of which expired in 2002, Mr. Greenspan urged Congress to adopt a mechanism that would allow for a "midcourse correction" in the event that budget deficits turn out to be sharply higher than expected.

That is another idea that the White House and Republican legislators have previously rejected, and it is one that is unlikely to be embraced this year.

Representative Jim Nussle, Republican of Iowa and chairman of the House Budget Committee, immediately took issue with Mr. Greenspan on the need for restrictions on future tax cuts.

"I would hate to see an arbitrary rule," Mr. Nussle said, noting that Democrats had bitterly opposed Mr. Bush's proposal to reduce taxes on dividends and capital gains—a tax cut that Mr. Greenspan endorsed in 2003 and said on Wednesday should be made permanent.

But Mr. Greenspan stood firm, contending that the "overriding" principle was to reduce the deficit and that Congress should find ways to pay for the cost of making the tax cuts permanent.

"Differing people hold differing views, and compromise is essential in getting a functioning legislature to work its will," Mr. Greenspan said.

In his testimony on Wednesday, Mr. Greenspan repeated his strong support for a crucial element of Mr. Bush's plan to replace part of Social Security with a system of private savings accounts.

Indeed, Mr. Greenspan implied the need for much bigger cuts than Mr. Bush has suggested in the government's full array of old-age entitlement programs, including Medicare as well as Social Security.

"I fear that we may have already committed more fiscal resources to the baby boom generation in its retirement years than our economy has the capacity to deliver," he told lawmakers. "If existing promises need to be changed, those changes should be made sooner rather than later."

Two Fed Officials Offer Different but Upbeat Views on Debt

By EDMUND L. ANDREWS—March 11, 2005

WASHINGTON, March 10—Two top Federal Reserve officials argued on Thursday that the United States' record level of foreign indebtedness was unlikely to pose a major risk to the nation.

"The resolution of our current-account deficit and household debt burdens does not strike me as overly worrisome," said Alan Greenspan, chairman of the Federal Reserve Board, according to a transcript of a speech he gave to the Council on Foreign Relations in New York.

In his most sanguine remarks yet on the subject, Mr. Greenspan repeated many of his previous arguments that increased globalization of trade and finance allows the United States to borrow much more today than it could comfortably have done two decades ago.

While cautioning that "the free lunch has yet to be invented," Mr. Greenspan nonetheless said the world was undergoing a "one-time shift in the degree of globalization and innovation that has temporarily altered the specific calibrations" for evaluating economic imbalances.

A member of the Fed board of governors, Ben S. Bernanke, went even further than Mr. Greenspan by attributing the United States' huge and rising foreign indebtedness to a "savings glut" in Asia and most other parts of the world, according

to a transcript of his speech to the Virginia Association of Economists in Richmond.

The fairly upbeat Fed assessments ran counter to those of some outside analysts, who warn that the nation's soaring trade and financial deficits could lead to a severe drop in the value of the dollar and perhaps to higher interest rates.

Investors have become extraordinarily nervous about the dollar in recent weeks, selling at any hint that Asian central banks might be ready to reduce the huge supplies of dollar-denominated securities that they built up to keep their own currencies from rising too rapidly.

Analysts estimate that the nation's trade deficit soared to more than $600 billion last year, or nearly 6 percent of gross domestic product. The nation's aggregate foreign indebtedness is now equal to more than one-fifth of the total economy.

Most economists expect the trade deficit and the broader current-account deficit, which includes capital flows as well as trade, to widen further because the American economy is growing faster than those of Europe and Japan.

Mr. Greenspan said the imbalance could not keep widening indefinitely. But he said the United States could now attract far more money than in the past because

globalization had greatly reduced "home bias"—the tendency of people to invest primarily in their own countries.

"Globalization—the extension of the division of labor and specialization beyond national borders—is patently a key to understanding much of our recent economic history," Mr. Greenspan said.

Though Mr. Greenspan acknowledged that globalization had its limits, he said it was impossible to know how long the trend could continue. "The closing of our frontier at the end of the 19th century, for example, did not signal the onset of a new era of economic stagnation," he remarked.

Mr. Bernanke, a former professor of economics at Princeton, offered a more unconventional view. Rather than ascribe the widening payments gap to the low rate of American savings or to booming competition from China, Mr. Bernanke attributed it to a huge pool of savings in developing nations around the world.

"Over the past decade, a combination of diverse forces has created a significant increase in the global supply of saving—a global saving glut," Mr. Bernanke said.

He added that the "glut" was in part the result of the Asian and Latin American financial crises of the mid-1990's. Many countries became net exporters of capital at that time, as investors looked for better places to put their money and central banks built up "war chests" to buffer themselves against future shocks.

Mr. Bernanke acknowledged that this shift could pose problems for the United States at some point. The flood of foreign imports has led to a "shrinkage" of American manufacturing and its potential for exports, he said. But like the Fed chairman, Mr. Bernanke said the imbalances would gradually readjust on their own. and added, "I see no reason the process should not proceed smoothly."

In Reply to Tightening of Sanctions, Castro Bans the Yankee Dollar

By GINGER THOMPSON—October 27, 2004

MEXICO CITY, Oct. 26—In a televised address, President Fidel Castro of Cuba announced Monday night that United States dollars, which have kept his country's ailing economy afloat for the past decade, would be banned from all commercial transactions in two weeks.

In his speech, Mr. Castro called the measure a response to the Bush administration's decisions to strengthen economic sanctions by placing new limits on the amount of money people can send to relatives in Cuba and imposing multi-million-dollar fines against banks that have transferred dollars to Cuba.

His aides said Cuba was "protecting itself from external economic aggression," and they asked Cubans to tell their relatives to send euros, British pounds or Canadian dollars.

After the fall of the Soviet Union in 1991 sent the Cuban economy into a tailspin, the government legalized United States dollars as a way of attracting foreign investment and remittances. Since then the government has become dependent on dollars to buy everything from oil to food and medical supplies. Its people rely on an esti-mated $1 billion a year from relatives in the United States.

After Nov. 8, though, stores, restaurants and other businesses will only accept a national currency known as the convertible peso, which has no value outside Cuba. Banks will end dollar transactions and convert dollar accounts to pesos. Officials announced that the government would charge Cubans a 10 percent fee to exchange dollars for pesos; there will be no fee to change other currencies to pesos.

Diplomats and other political analysts saw the measures as more pragmatic than philosophical.

Some analysts said that by forcing Cubans to turn in their dollars, Mr. Castro's government could then use the currency to buy needed food and fuel on the international market.

In recent weeks the country has suffered serious shortages of electricity. Blackouts are common most afternoons in neighborhoods across the capital. Several hotels have been forced to close for days at a time, and public pressure had grown so intense that Mr. Castro fired the minister of industry, who was considered a close political ally.

"I don't think this is a political decision at all," said Ricardo Pascoe, Mexico's former ambassador to Cuba. "It's a pragmatic move. Cuba has to buy more oil than it had planned, and so it urgently needs dollars."

Marifeli Pérez-Stable of the InterAmerican Dialogue, a policy institute in Washington, said Mr. Castro was using the American sanctions as a chance to seize more control over the Cuban economy. "The Bush administration played right into his hands," she said, by giving him an excuse to justify "exercising greater control over the population."

In Washington, The Associated Press quoted a State Department spokesman as saying the ban on dollars proved that Mr. Bush's policies were working. "We think this is yet another indicator that Castro is refusing to do what's best for his own people," said the spokesman, Adam Ereli. "It shows that he is cynically trying to preserve a bankrupt regime at his people's expense."

Across Havana, people lined up outside banks to get more information on the new policy and convert dollars to pesos. The banks are to stay open on Saturday and Sunday.

While making his announcement, Mr. Castro, 78, wore a sling on his right arm and a cast on his left leg, results of his public fall after a speech five days ago. Since the accident, Mr. Castro has taken pains to show he is still in control of the government, including insisting on staying conscious during surgery.

As Rates Climb, the Short-Term C.D. Is Standing Taller

By NORM ALSTER—September 04, 2005

ATTENTION, prudent savers. You can now risk a peek at your financial statements.

As the Federal Reserve has continued to raise short-term interest rates, returns on money market funds and short-term bank certificates of deposit have been climbing back to respectability. After several years in which Fed policies have tended to benefit spenders, borrowers and investors, now savers are getting their day in the sun.

Many money market funds, which just over a year ago were returning a negligible 0.7 percent, are now inching toward 3.5 percent. And at some banks, savers can now earn close to 4.5 percent on 12-month certificates of deposit, a return that is more than the 4.04 percent yield of the 10-year Treasury note. Many people expect the Fed to raise rates at least one or two more times, so more good news is likely. "It's the first time in a long time savers will benefit," said Jim McDonald, who manages money market funds at T. Rowe Price.

But after a tough couple of decades, savers have a lot of ground to make up.

While stock investors feasted on the long bull market of the 1980's and 90's, savers were pretty much left in the dust. With the massacre of stocks in 2000 and 2001, many savers reasoned that their time had finally come. But Alan Greenspan, the Fed chairman, opted to pump money into the economy, repeatedly cutting rates and sending yields on short-term vehicles like savings and checking accounts, money market funds and some C.D.'s into basement-level single digits. Indeed, Mr. McDonald said, for much of the last year, inflation-adjusted returns for many savers have been below zero, meaning that savers were in essence paying financial institutions to use their dollars. By contrast, low rates were a boon to spenders and to borrowers making major purchases like homes and cars. They also improved the outlook for investors by easing balance-sheet pressures on corporations.

But since June of last year, Mr. Greenspan has changed course, raising rates 10 times and bemoaning the disinclination of Americans to save. Money market returns, typically with a six-week lag, have mirrored the rate climb. Hence, the T. Rowe Price Summit Cash Reserves fund, with a current seven-day yield of 3.14 percent, is expected to rise an additional 10 basis points, or hundredths of a percentage point, over the next few weeks to reflect the Fed's latest rate bump. Mr. McDonald expects that future increases by the Fed could push money returns toward 5 percent by the middle of next year. "The marketplace expects two more 25-basis-point hikes this year. We think the Fed is going to do more than the marketplace is pricing in," he said.

While yields on longer term government bonds remain stubbornly low, the rising rates for money markets and short-term C.D.'s have begun to attract new dollars. Dennis Miars, a real estate developer and investor in San Dimas, Calif., about 25 miles east of Los Angeles, has prospered during the housing boom, but he recently sold his investments in rental properties and has been buying bank certificates of deposit. "We're finding the C.D. rates are starting to go up and the real estate market is starting to slow down," Mr. Miars said.

Ashwin Adarkar, executive vice president at IndyMac Bank, which is based in Pasadena, Calif., and has 22 branches, said that "more and more people are getting off the sidelines." C.D. deposits at IndyMac, which is now offering a one-year certificate at a compounded rate of 4.2 percent, have doubled over the last year, to $4.6 billion, Mr. Adarkar said.

At Nexity Bank in Birmingham, Ala., Donald Long, its president, reported a "marked increase" in C.D. purchases. Nexity is now offering a 12-month C.D. at 4.3 percent. And at T. Rowe Price, money market fund assets have climbed by roughly $750 million—on a base of $10.7 billion—since January.

Over all, the flow of cash into money market funds has risen in each of the last three months, the first such string of gains since 2002, according to Lipper, the mutual fund tracker. Until recently, said Donald Cassidy, senior research analyst at Lipper, investors seemed to have a "cash is trash" attitude. Now, money funds are attracting cash and equity funds are treading water. Despite the fact that July was a good month for shares, Mr. Cassidy said, flow into equity funds was flat, apart from rising 401(k) distributions.

A rate of 4 percent may not seem all that attractive to investors who expect stocks to do better. But the flow of money into money market funds may itself augur poorly for stock returns.

K. Geert Rouwenhorst, professor of finance at the Yale School of Management, has studied the daily flows of cash into money market and equity funds and found a negative correlation between the two. On days when money pours into stocks, it tends to come out of money market funds, and vice versa. "People often switch between money market and equity funds assets," said Professor Rouwenhorst.

It may not be surprising that investors, who often use money market funds as checking accounts for stock purchases, would shift money between money market and equity funds. But can sustained flows into money markets actually predict impending declines in equity investment?

Andrew Clark, a mathematician and senior research analyst at Lipper, has concluded that they can. "There is predictive value when money starts flowing into money market funds," Mr. Clark said. "Increased investment in money market funds tends to have a dampening effect on equity fund investment." The possibility of investor disinterest leading to flat or sinking stock equity markets makes that 3.5 to 4.5 percent yield even more attractive.

Already, many savers are beneficiaries of a curious anomaly that allows them to earn returns that equal or exceed those of long-term investors in Treasury securities. Typically, long-term returns are much higher as investors must be rewarded for locking up their assets over a longer period. But the differential between long and short term rates—known as the yield curve—has flattened, a phenomenon that Mr. Greenspan has called a "conundrum." The Fed has been raising short-term rates but does not control long-term rates, and these have simply not tracked higher.

What could sour this rare moment of triumph for savers? A significant housing slowdown would curtail mortgage loan demand and eliminate some of the jockeying among banks to attract assets with high C.D. rates. And a slowing of the overall economy would cause the Fed to stop raising, or to even begin lowering rates.

One final threat comes from abroad. Dollar-rich foreign central banks, particularly those of China, Japan, South Korea and Taiwan, have been major buyers of long-term Treasuries. What if these giant lenders, mindful of increasingly appealing short-term rates, start shifting more of their assets into short-term instruments? "If there was a concerted effort by foreign central banks to buy more short-term Treasuries, that could depress short-term rates and raise long-term rates," said Mr. Clark, the Lipper analyst.

But Mr. Miars, the California real estate developer, isn't worried. "I'm advising my kids to pick up C.D.'s," he said.

The Doctrine Was Not to Have One

By EDMUND L. ANDREWS—August 26, 2005

JACKSON HOLE, Wyo., Aug. 25—Alan Greenspan was at the height of his success as chairman of the Federal Reserve in November 1999: the economy was booming, inflation was negligible and people at all levels were becoming wealthier.

But even as Mr. Greenspan was being celebrated as the economy's "maestro," he sounded far less omniscient behind closed doors.

"We really do not know how this system works," he told members of the Fed's policy-making committee in Washington, according to transcripts released earlier this year. "It's clearly new. The old models just are not working."

Now, as he nears the end of his 18-year tenure in the job, Mr. Greenspan is leaving a brilliant record but a murky legacy.

Despite numerous economic shocks and financial excesses, unemployment and inflation are both lower now than many economists considered possible when Mr. Greenspan took office in 1987. But whoever moves into his spacious office on Constitution Avenue early next year faces a near-impossible task in replicating Mr. Greenspan's success in managing monetary policy.

That is because Mr. Greenspan abhorred rules, was skeptical about economic models and jettisoned practices that were enshrined by the likes of Paul A. Volcker, his predecessor, and Milton Friedman, a winner of the Nobel in economic science. If Mr. Greenspan stood for anything, it was flexibility and the freedom from dogma.

"The Greenspan standard has for the most part meant what Greenspan wanted to do," said Alan S. Blinder, a professor of economics at Princeton and a former vice chairman of the Federal Reserve.

Mr. Blinder will be one of many economists at a Federal Reserve symposium beginning here Friday that will be devoted to discussions about the "post-Greenspan era." Before that, however, the gathering will open with what is expected to be Mr. Greenspan's swan song speech as chairman of the Fed.

Mr. Greenspan, whose term as a Fed governor expires in January and cannot be renewed, is thought likely to devote his speech to the lessons he learned running the central bank longer than all but one of his predecessors, William McChesney Martin Jr. Expected to be listening particularly closely at the conference are three of the leading candidates to succeed him: Ben S. Bernanke, President Bush's chief economic adviser; Martin S. Feldstein, an economist at Harvard; and R. Glenn Hubbard of Columbia University.

But for all his triumphs, Mr. Greenspan also presided over a stock market bubble that burst and, in helping minimize the damage from that fiasco, laid the ground-work for the housing boom—and potential bust—that followed.

Moreover, the United States has run up heavy foreign debt partly because the Federal Reserve drove interest rates so low that Americans borrowed more and saved less.

Mr. Greenspan's approach to such challenges was to roll with the punches, basing his management of the economy on a refusal to believe in firm rules, doctrines or models.

"A surprising problem is that a number of economists are not able to distinguish between the economic models we construct and the real world," he remarked back in 1984, when he was still head of a private consulting firm.

As Fed chairman, Mr. Greenspan has celebrated the hunt for "anomalies" or trends that seemed to defy what the models predict. He had little faith in widely accepted concepts like the "natural rate" of unemployment, which many economists long believed to be about 6 percent.

He jettisoned the practice of basing policy on growth in the money supply, a concept enshrined by Mr. Friedman as the best way to prevent inflation.

And though he has cultivated the reputation of a hard-liner on reducing inflation, Mr. Greenspan has often put more emphasis on driving up employment.

At 78, his hair is thinning and his gait is becoming stiffer. But he may be as famous as any pop star;

he is certainly a larger-than-life figure for political leaders and economists. At a hearing in July before the House Financial Services Committee, lawmakers from both parties showered him with so much praise that they began running out of accolades.

"All the adjectives have been used up," complained Representative Steve Pearce, Republican of New Mexico, who then declared that Mr. Greenspan was a "handsome man."

By almost all accounts, Mr. Greenspan has been an exceptionally successful steward for the economy. In the last 18 years, the nation has endured only two recessions, one of them quite mild. There were four downturns in the previous 18 years.

The core rate of inflation has edged down to about 2 percent from 4 percent when he took office. Unemployment has averaged 5.5 percent over the last 18 years, compared with nearly 7 percent in the previous 18 years, and it is now down to about 5 percent.

Mr. Blinder, a Democrat who battled with Mr. Greenspan over the Fed's communication policy, said his former boss might well be the best central banker who ever lived.

Allen Sinai, chief global economist at Decision Economics, pointed to one reason Mr. Greenspan was so willing to rely on his gut instincts. "He didn't go to one of the top schools: Harvard or M.I.T. or Stanford or Northwestern," Mr. Sinai said. "I think that was an advantage. He didn't get brainwashed into one of the doctrines."

A devout believer in free markets and at one time a disciple of Ayn Rand, the libertarian philosopher, Mr. Greenspan—who studied at New York University—served as chairman of the Council of Economic Advisers under President Gerald R. Ford. As head of Townsend-Greenspan, the forecasting firm he ran both before and after his White House years, Mr. Greenspan made his reputation by poring through vast amounts of industry data to tease out economic trends.

Named by President Ronald Reagan to succeed Mr. Volcker as Fed chairman in 1987, Mr. Greenspan brought both his passion for detail and a cool head for crises.

The first crisis arrived barely two months after he arrived when the stock market crashed more than 500 points on Oct. 19, 1987.

Mr. Greenspan, initially mistrusted as a weak successor to the iron-willed Mr. Volcker, quickly soothed the economy by assuring banks that the Fed would provide enough money to keep financial markets functioning. With the Fed offering money to all takers, interest rates edged down, markets recovered and the crash turned out to be little more than a pause in the bull market.

Years later, Mr. Greenspan said one of his proudest achievements was the fact that he had been able to sleep the night after Black Monday.

But Mr. Greenspan gradually ushered in a host of more enduring changes at the Fed. With memories of the 1970's era of soaring prices still strong, he initiated "preemptive" changes in interest rates to head off inflation before it actually arrived, calling the practice "leaning against the wind."

By relentlessly raising interest rates in 1989, the Fed contributed to an unexpectedly sharp economic downturn that played a major role in the election defeat of the first President Bush in 1992. The second attempt, a sharp rise in rates in 1994 and 1995, went more smoothly: inflation remained low, the economy cooled briefly and then began its biggest growth spurt in decades.

Many economists say Mr. Greenspan's signal triumph was being among the first to recognize that starting in the mid-1990's, the United States had entered a sustained period of faster productivity growth. The increase had profound implications, because it meant that the economy could grow faster and unemployment could fall lower than had ever seemed possible without fueling inflation.

The productivity shift was not apparent in official government statistics, and Mr. Greenspan found himself bucking his own staff economists as well as Fed governors like Janet Yellen and Laurence H. Meyer.

At the time, most economists assumed inflation would heat up once unemployment dipped below 5.5 percent. But Mr. Greenspan, convinced that investments in computers and information technology were finally paying off in faster productivity, was content to let unemployment sink to less than 4 percent. "He was confident in his judgment and he was right," Mr. Blinder said. "The lesson is that sometimes you can't wait for the data to be definitive."

Some economists point to an even broader legacy for future Fed policy. Before Mr. Greenspan took over, they note, policy makers focused almost entirely on changes in demand as the determinant of inflation. The surge in productivity showed that changes on the economy's supply side could be equally, if not more, important.

Critics of Mr. Greenspan contend that he has relied too heavily on his own judgment and not enough on consistent principles.

"We've moved further away from a rules-based system," said Brian S. Wesbury, chief investment strategist at Claymore Advisers. "We have a Greenspan standard, but we don't have any kind of a Fed standard."

If the Fed had adopted an explicit numerical inflation target—something that many other central banks use but that Mr. Greenspan has rejected as too restrictive—Mr. Wesbury contended that the Fed might have avoided much of the volatility since 2000.

With little inflation in sight, the Fed might have raised interest rates less than it did in 1999, which might have softened the downturn that followed. That in turn might have made the Fed less eager to drive down rates when the stock market fell sharply in 2000, causing less of a potential bubble in housing prices today.

Other analysts contend that Mr. Greenspan's judgment has generally been correct, but that the Fed cannot afford to rely on the individual judgment of future chairmen.

"If you are Alan Greenspan, it's hard to make a rule that would do any better," said Allen H. Meltzer, professor of economics at Carnegie Mellon University and author of a history of the Fed. "On the other hand, we have had 12 chairmen at the Federal Reserve since 1913, and some of them have made massive blunders."

Mr. Greenspan remains convinced that the economy is simply too complex and fast moving to be subject to a single policy rule or predictable with any single economic model. If he has one consistent message, it is that nothing is permanent.

While many economists warn that the United States has become dangerously loaded up with foreign debt, Mr. Greenspan has argued that the globalization of finance and other changes may have created a global "savings glut" that allows the United States to borrow much more than would have been possible 20 years ago.

His alternative to firm rules is "risk management," a strategy of making policy based on a range of possible outcomes. The clearest example came in 2003, when the Fed worried about the slim possibility of a broad deflation, a downward spiral in consumer prices.

Though Fed officials viewed deflation as highly unlikely, they figured the damage would be heavy if it did occur. Mr. Greenspan cut short-term rates to 1 percent in 2003, then promised to keep them at that level for a "considerable period" that turned out to be a year.

The biggest risk for his successor could turn out to be a collapse in housing prices after the frenetic run-up that has resulted in part from the Fed's policy of keeping interest rates so low. But another key principle of the Greenspan Fed, which most experts have come to accept, is that the central bank should focus on economic fundamentals and not try to prematurely pop a market bubble in stock prices or real estate prices.

After the stock market bubble burst in 2000, Mr. Greenspan argued that the Fed would have made a mistake if it had tried to curb speculation by raising interest rates or making it harder for investors to buy stock with borrowed money.

It was better, he argued, to fix things afterward by cutting interest rates. With evidence of speculative excess in many housing markets, Mr. Greenspan is now warning that investors may be overconfident that interest rates will stay low and that housing prices will continue to soar.

But if housing prices do turn out to be a bubble that bursts, trapping homeowners who used exotic new mortgages to borrow far more than was once allowed, Mr. Greenspan will no longer be around to take the blame—or clean up the mess.

The Fed Steps Up Interest Rates a Sixth Time

By EDMUND L. ANDREWS—February 03, 2005

WASHINGTON, Feb. 2—The Federal Reserve raised short-term interest rates on Wednesday, its sixth increase since June, and signaled that it intends to keep raising rates in the months to come.

The central bank nudged the federal funds rate, the rate charged on overnight loans between banks, by a quarter of a point, to 2.5 percent.

In a statement that accompanied Wednesday's decision, the policy-setting Federal Open Market Committee repeated previous declarations that it could afford to raise rates at "a pace that is likely to be measured." By echoing its policy statement from December almost word for word, the Fed indicated that it has not yet developed a plan to either accelerate or pause in its slow-but-steady approach to raising rates in small increments at each meeting. Policymakers also stuck to their relatively sanguine outlook on the economy, saying that growth appeared to be solid and inflation expectations were "well-contained."

Since starting to tighten policy, the Fed has more than doubled overnight lending rates from their near-record low of 1 percent eight months ago. Even with the latest rate increase, short-term borrowing costs are barely equal to the pace of inflation and still well below historical averages. More important, long-term interest rates for corporate bonds and home mortgages have declined in recent months.

Analysts said there was so much money available for lending that financial institutions were reducing margins on loans for relatively high-risk corporate borrowers.

"There is so much liquidity in the marketplace that the only way lending institutions can compete is by lowering rates," said William Zadrozny, chief executive of Siemens Financial Services, which provides financing for business equipment and an array of other needs. "People are reaching to employ their money."

The Fed's decision had little impact on stock and bond markets, because investors viewed the rate increase as a foregone conclusion.

The Standard " Poor's 500 index rose slightly after the announcement, and investors continued to snap up long-term Treasury bonds in the expectation that inflation and interest rates would remain relatively low.

The confidence of bond investors continues to surprise many analysts.

The spread between interest rates for risk-free 10-year Treasury bonds and riskier corporate bonds is at its narrowest since 1998, according to data compiled by Richard Yamarone, chief economist at Argus Research, an economic consulting firm in New York.

"It's too much money chasing too few goods," said Mr. Yamarone, harking back to the description of inflation originally coined by the economist Milton Friedman.

The spread between rates on 10-year Treasury bonds and corporate junk bonds—those rated below Baa by Moody's Investors Service—has declined from 3.01 percent in March 2001 to 1.76 percent as of last week.

Even though some Fed officials have begun to worry that rising costs to hire workers and slowing growth of productivity could fuel inflation, the central bank said on Wednesday that the upside and downside risks to both inflation and growth were still "roughly equal."

"Even after this action, the stance of monetary policy remains accommodative and, coupled with robust underlying growth in productivity, is providing ongoing support to economic activity," the committee said in its statement.

By reiterating that monetary policy is still "accommodative," the Fed signaled that interest rates had not yet reached a neutral level that neither encourages inflation nor slows down the economy.

Alan Greenspan, chairman of the Fed, has refused to say what a neutral rate would be in practice. But most analysts expect the Fed to keep raising the overnight rate until it reaches at least 3.5 percent or perhaps 4 percent.

Mr. Greenspan is expected to shed more light about the Fed's plans when he testifies before House and Senate banking committees on Feb. 16 and Feb. 17.

Fed officials face several big uncertainties as they plot their interest-rate strategy. They need to dissect conflicting pressures on inflation: Consumer prices have climbed more slowly in recent months, but last year's increase in oil prices has not yet had its full impact.

Potentially more important, Fed officials must grapple with the possibility of a slowdown in productivity growth and rising costs to hire workers.

Faster productivity growth allows the nation to produce more goods and expand more rapidly than would otherwise be possible without sparking higher inflation.

The nation's productivity soared at a pace of more than 4 percent a year in 2002 and 2003, nearly twice as fast as economists consider normal for the United States, but it slowed to 1.8 percent in the third quarter of 2004 and may have declined even more since then.

Economists say it is normal for productivity to rise in the early stages of an economic recovery, as companies try to meet rising demand for goods without adding more workers. Improvements in productivity usually slow down in the later stages of a recovery as employers pay higher wages to recruit scarce workers.

Faster productivity growth allowed Mr. Greenspan to defy conventional wisdom in the middle and late 1990's by keeping interest rates relatively low even though the economy was booming. But Fed officials are already wondering whether the pace will stabilize at the relatively strong rate of about 2.5 percent that became normal in the late 1990's.

Ben S. Bernanke, a Fed governor, gave a detailed analysis of the issue in a speech last month and cautiously sided with optimists who predict that productivity will remain at its late 1990's levels.

"I think the productivity optimists have a good case," Mr. Bernanke said, citing research that showed that technological advances would continue to spread throughout the economy even if the overall pace of technological advance slows somewhat.

But William Dudley, chief United States economist at Goldman Sachs, warned last week that productivity might slow more than many analysts predict.

Among other potential drags on productivity, Mr. Dudley cited the federal government's large and stubborn budget deficits that drain capital from private investment, the need for companies to divert more money into energy-saving equipment and a slowing pace of technological change.

Mr. Greenspan appeared to signal that he remains open to both sides of this debate.

An Uneven Fight Against Inflation

By DANIEL ALTMAN—August 28, 2005

INFLATION is rising in virtually all of the world's big economies, but not all central banks are fighting it actively. Local economic conditions supply the obvious excuse for this behavior. Yet, looking at history, one can make a strong argument that controlling inflation should trump those concerns.

To track inflation, governments usually release two sets of figures: the overall change in prices, and a rate of change that excludes volatile food and energy prices. Lately, the second figure has often been quite a bit lower than the first, because of sharp upsurges in the prices of oil and a few other commodities.

That second figure, however, provides only false comfort. Economists worry about inflation because of the cycle it sets in motion. People have to pay more for the goods and services they buy, so they demand higher wages. Businesses see their labor costs rise, so they raise the prices of their products. Then workers demand higher wages again, and so on.

This cycle has some nasty side effects. The local currency loses value in world markets, so consumers can no longer afford imports. Companies have to redo their pricing schedules, so long-term contracts become difficult to impossible. Credit markets suffer under the weight of high interest rates, which lenders require to offset the dwindling value of the currency. The fact that part of the current inflation comes from oil and food doesn't change this process.

That's not to say prices are already in an inescapable skyward spiral. The most recent inflation figures for the United States, Britain and the euro area are all less than 4 percent for the last 12 months. With a target of about 2 percent broadly accepted among central bankers—the Bank of England and the European Central Bank set it explicitly—that's probably within an acceptable margin.

But there are grounds for caution. Just because you have a 2 percent target doesn't mean that you expect inflation to be above and below that target for equal periods of time, as some analysts have suggested.

Simply put, the causes and costs of being on either side of the target are not the same. An economy may sustain lower-than-target inflation for years as a result of rapid improvements in workers' productivity, which allow the same products to be made for less money. While zero or negative inflation can be a persistent problem, as it has been in Japan until recently, such readings have historically been a transitory phenomenon. The same can't be said for inflation of about 3.5 percent or higher, which tends to persist or even float upward.

Moreover, price increases are accelerating when considered on a monthly basis. Part of the movement may be seasonal, at least in the United States, but these rates show a definite upward tilt.

Though they have all experienced similar upturns in prices, three major central banks have responded in different ways. In the euro area, there has been essentially no reaction; handcuffed by worries about two of its biggest member economies, Germany and Italy, the European Central Bank has kept short-term interest rates steady. In Britain, concerns that a 12-year spell of uninterrupted growth may soon end have led the Bank of England to lower rates. And in the United States, the Federal Reserve has sent short-term rates steadily higher, though without much effect on the long-term rates faced by most consumers.

The Fed has been lucky, in a sense, because it has been able to put itself in a better inflation-fighting position without damaging the economy. But inflation of 5 percent in the first half of the year, or 4 percent when adjusted for seasonal changes, offers a powerful reason for the Fed to grab the private sector's attention. To do that, it may have to raise short-term interest rates by more than a quarter of a percentage point at a time.

The European Central Bank has less excuse for reticence. Its main mission is to keep prices stable and, as such, it is licensed to prop up economic growth only when there is a danger of falling prices. Undoubtedly, the weak conditions in the euro area have created pressure on the bank to keep rates steady or even to cut them. The bank's independence, however, is intended to make it immune from such pressure.

The Bank of England's posture looks to be the most perilous of the three. Despite sagging retail sales, the British economy has been growing at an annual rate of 1.7 percent, adjusted for inflation—a rate that Germans and Italians may envy. Unemployment is still very low, at about 5 percent. By cutting rates, the central bank seems to be acting pre-emptively—and that's putting it kindly—to head off economic weakness.

By contrast, the threat of inflation is already present in all three economic regions. True, unemployment could join with inflation to form the deadly combination known as stagflation, which dogged the United States and other wealthy countries during the oil shocks of the 1970's and has ruined many developing economies since then. But the historically proven solution to stagflation is not to cut interest rates and hope for growth and jobs; it is to raise rates and wait for prices to even out.

Monetary policy has moved on quite a bit since the 1970's. One wouldn't expect any of the three banks to allow inflation to hit the double digits, as it did as recently as the early 1990's in some euro area countries. Still, caution never goes out of style.

A Painful Goodbye to Cheap Money

By DANIEL ALTMAN—November 21, 2004

MONEY doesn't grow on trees, though for a while there it seemed as if it did.

Americans had years to get used to zero-percent financing on cars and major appliances, rock-bottom mortgages and cut-rate credit card deals. They borrowed prodigiously to pay for more spending, even when paychecks weren't growing and neither was employment. As tepid and intermittent as the economy's recovery from the 2001 recession has been, it owes a big part of its very existence to that American willingness to go on consuming, come what may.

But in raising short-term interest rates to 2 percent this month, with more increases likely to come, the Federal Reserve has signaled that the days of arboreal money are over. Americans are going to start feeling the cost of repaying their debts.

The adjustment could be a painful one. No longer will many consumers be able to make impulse buys—a new stereo, washing machine or sports coupe—with no payments due for a year or more. Credit card companies will no longer come knocking with dazzling balance-transfer offers.

Time that used to be spent hunting for a new home, spurred on by record low mortgage rates, may be devoted instead to finding a good I.R.A. or mutual fund to house the down-payment money. And some people who are already living on the knife edge between managing their monthly payments and falling into bankruptcy will be pushed over the edge.

Short-term interest rates are going up now for two reasons: because the specter of inflation is returning as the economy resumes a path of steady growth, and because the Fed needs some room to maneuver in case that path turns out not to be so steady.

Inflation hasn't become a problem so far, but there are some signs in the data that it may. Last month, the prices that businesses pay for labor and materials rose by a whopping 1.7 percent; consumer prices rose, too, though more moderately. There is not much sign in the latest statistics that productivity growth is helping to moderate inflation, so it is likely that the Fed will have to go on raising rates to head it off.

It won't take long before households feel the pinch: their payments on existing loans with adjustable rates will go up, and new borrowing will cost them more. Since many credit cards today charge floating rates linked to the prime rate, which moves in lock-step with the Fed, some of this squeeze is already occurring.

Higher credit-card rates are likely to result in less borrowing, said David B. Gross, vice president of Lexecon, an economic consulting firm in Chicago. "Certainly, you would see some substantial effect within a year," he said.

Research that Mr. Gross published in 2002 with Nicholas S. Souleles of the University of Pennsylvania showed that a 10 percent increase in credit card rates—say, a bump up to a 6.5 percent rate from 5.9 percent before—was associated with a drop of 13 percent in borrowing. Less borrowing usually means less spending, and that could take much of the consumer wind out of the economy's sails.

The situation differs for mortgages and other long-term loans. Rates on most of those are fixed, said Robert E. Mellman, a senior economist at J. P. Morgan Chase, so few existing borrowers are threatened. But with higher rates making the payments larger on new loans, some house and car buyers may have to choose between settling for a smaller purchase and not buying at all.

Less demand for housing, in particular, could also lead to lower spending in other areas of the economy. If house prices fall, homeowners may feel less wealthy and spend less of their incomes—the so-called wealth effect working in reverse. And the combination of falling house prices and rising rates could close off one of the most important sources of fresh spending cash for consumers in recent years: refinancings and home-equity loans.

Mortgage rates are generally linked to long-term bond rates, and have not yet reflected the Fed's moves. But if the Fed keeps raising short-term rates, lenders will have to start charging more, too. Mr. Mellman said that he and his colleagues expect long-term rates to start rising in 2005.

ALL this matters more than ever to most Americans because they owe so much. Fed statistics for the first half of the year show that households' debt payments stood near an all-time high, as a share of after-tax income. The recent pickup in the economy may have offset the effects of the Fed's first few moves to raise rates, by raising average incomes enough to keep pace. But that may not last, because several factors could combine to push long-term rates up sharply.

One factor is the federal budget deficit. Financial markets may shrug off a bad year or two, but when expectations grow for a long string of big deficits—caused, for example, by big permanent tax cuts or costly overseas conflicts that last longer than expected—the government's need to borrow can drive up rates for everyone.

Interest rates could also climb if factors like a weak dollar and slowing consumer demand make America a less attractive place for the world to invest, or if, conversely, something suddenly went very right—say, a technological breakthrough that caused a sudden spike in the demand for capital to exploit it.

Indeed, higher long-term rates could be a sign that the economy is ready to grow faster: a booming economy brings more demand for credit, which can drive up rates, but it also brings the threat of rapid inflation, which can compel the Fed to put on the brakes by raising rates. That in turn could herald an economic slowdown, with stagnant incomes and widening unemployment—a potentially devastating cocktail for heavily indebted Americans.

Daniel Altman is the author of "Neoconomy: George Bush's Revolutionary Gamble With America's Future."

A Whiff of Stagflation

By PAUL KRUGMAN—April 18, 2005

IN the 1970's soaring prices of oil and other commodities led to stagflation—a combination of high inflation and high unemployment, which left no good policy options. If the Fed cut interest rates to create jobs, it risked causing an inflationary spiral; if it raised interest rates to bring inflation down, it would further increase unemployment.

Can it happen again?

Last week fears of a return to stagflation sent stock prices to a five-month low. What few seem to have noticed, however, is that a mild form of stagflation—rising inflation in an economy still well short of full employment—has already arrived.

True, measured unemployment isn't bad by historical standards, and inflation is in the low single digits. But inflation is creeping up, and it's doing so despite a labor market that is in worse shape than the official unemployment rate suggests.

Let's start with the jobs picture. The official unemployment rate is 5.2 percent—roughly equal to the average for the Clinton years.

But unemployment statistics only count those who are actively looking for jobs. Every other indicator shows a situation much less favorable to workers than that of the 1990's. A lower fraction of the adult population is employed; the average duration of unemployment—a rough indicator of how long it takes laid-off workers to find new jobs—is much higher than it was in the 1990's.

Above all, the weak job market leaves workers with no bargaining power, so they aren't getting ahead: wage increases have been minimal, and haven't kept up with inflation.

Underlying these disappointing numbers is sluggish job creation. Private-sector employment is still lower than it was before the 2001 recession.

Things could be, and have been, worse. But those whose standard of living depends on wages, not capital gains—in other words, the vast majority of Americans—aren't feeling particularly prosperous. By two to one, people tell pollsters that the economy is "only fair" or "poor," not "good" or "excellent."

Why, then, has the Fed been raising interest rates? Because it is worried about inflation, which has risen to the top end of the 2 to 3 percent range the Fed prefers.

What's driving inflation? Not wages: labor costs have been falling, because wages are growing less than productivity. Oil prices are a big part of the story, but not all of it. Other commodity prices are also rising; health care costs are once again on the march. And a combination of capacity shortages, rising Asian demand and a weakening dollar has given industries like cement and steel new "pricing power."

It all adds up to a mild case of stagflation: inflation is leading the Fed to tap on the brakes, even though this doesn't look or feel like a full-employment economy.

We shouldn't overstate the case: we're not back to the economic misery of the 1970's. But the fact that we're already experiencing mild stagflation means that there will be no good options if something else goes wrong.

Suppose, for example, that the consumer pullback visible in recent data turns out to be bigger than we now think, and growth stalls. (Not that long ago many economists thought that an oil price in the 50's would cause a recession.) Can the Fed stop raising interest rates and go back to rate cuts without causing the dollar to plunge and inflation to soar?

Or suppose that there's some kind of oil supply disruption—or that warnings about declining production from Saudi oil fields turn out to be right. Suppose that Asian central banks decide that they already have too many dollars. Suppose that the housing bubble bursts. Any of these events could easily turn our mild case of stagflation into something much more serious.

How do we get out of this bind? As the old joke goes, I wouldn't start from here. We should have spent the years of cheap oil encouraging conservation; we should have spent the years of modest growth in medical costs reforming our health care system. Oh, and we'd have a wider range of policy options if the budget weren't so deeply in deficit.

So if any of these things does come to pass, we'll just have to see how well an administration in which political operatives make all economic policy decisions, and the Treasury secretary is only a salesman, handles crises.

E-mail: krugman@nytimes.com

Two Mavericks in Economics Awarded Nobel Prize

By LOUIS UCHITELLE—October 12, 2004

AN American and a Norwegian economist were awarded the Nobel in economics yesterday for their efforts to demonstrate that innovative technologies and shocks, like a sharp increase in oil prices, play a much greater role in causing booms and recessions than fluctuations in demand.

The $1.3 million Nobel Memorial Prize in Economic Science went to Edward C. Prescott, 63, and Finn E. Kydland, 60, for two papers they wrote between 1977 and 1982. Their findings contradicted Keynesian theory, which held that changes in demand, particularly consumer demand, played the greatest role in business cycles. The Prescott-Kydland papers "transformed academic research in economics" and also transformed policy making, the Royal Swedish Academy of Sciences said in its citation.

Their first paper, which appeared when both were at Carnegie Mellon University in Pittsburgh, argued in effect that government officials should adhere to rules rather than resort to short-term policy shifts when circumstances change. If holding down inflation is the Federal Reserve's goal, for example, then the Fed should refrain from sharp cuts in interest rates during hard times, an approach that might result in too much stimulus and too much inflation later on. Better to resist changes in policy and suffer through some hardship if minimizing inflation makes people better off in the long run, their thesis maintained.

The two economists developed their second paper in the summer of 1980. Mr. Kydland had returned temporarily to his undergraduate alma mater, the Norwegian School of Economics and Business Administration in Bergen, and Mr. Prescott had gone there as a visiting professor with his wife and three children. Out of that collaboration came the view that supply shocks or new technology produce booms and busts, not changes in demand.

The two men, and Mr. Prescott in particular, "got people to think more broadly about what influences the economy over time," said Gary Stern, president of the Federal Reserve Bank of Minneapolis.

Mr. Prescott divides his time between a teaching post at Arizona State University and a staff job at the Federal Reserve Bank of Minneapolis, making him the first Nobel laureate employed by the Fed. From 1980 through 2003, he had served as an adviser to the Minneapolis bank while holding a regular job as a professor of economics at the University of Minnesota.

Mr. Kydland has taught almost continuously at Carnegie Mellon since 1978, but is on leave this academic year at the University of California, Santa Barbara.

There was one catch in their work that has riled a faction of the economics profession. The Prescott-Kydland finding assumed that demand was always at a high level. Everyone who wanted to work did so at the prevailing wage and all production could be sold at the existing market price. Supply, in effect, created its own demand. Thus, they posited, changes to the economy came not from fluctuations in demand, but from shocks.

The oil embargo that caused sharply higher prices and the 9/11 terrorism would be negative shocks, while the Internet and high-speed computers would have a positive impact, increasing productivity and growth. The negative supply shocks, and not policy, cut into consumer spending and job creation.

"Everyone thought that monetary policy shocks—sharp changes in interest rates—made economic growth fluctuate," Mr. Prescott said in a telephone interview yesterday. "We found, to our surprise, that persistent changes in real factors gave rise to fluctuations in the business cycle."

That thesis in the second paper was controversial because it went directly against the worldview of John Maynard Keynes, the famed British economist who held that the Depression was a result of weaker employment and weaker demand for the goods and services than the nation was capable of producing.

To make supply and demand balance each other at a high level, policy makers had to step in with sharply lower interest rates or increased public spending or well-aimed tax cuts, or some combination of the three.

That is still a strongly held view among some economists who criticized the Nobel award to Mr. Prescott and Mr. Kydland. "I am not alone in feeling that the Kydland-Prescott model of business cycles was a significant step backward," said Robert Gordon, an economist at Northwestern University.

The second paper was published at a time when Keynesian theory was in retreat, partly as a result of the stagflation, or rising inflation despite a weak economy, that appeared in the 1970's. Some economists argue that the Prescott-Kydland paper, rather than rule out demand as a cause of business cycle fluctuation, simply added supply shocks as an additional cause.

"What they did was layer supply shocks into the description of how the business cycle worked," said Achuthan Lakshman, managing director of the Economic Cycle Research Institute.

Mr. Gordon argued yesterday that numerous economists had already achieved this integration and the Prescott-Kydland paper followed in their footsteps, with the additional questionable thesis that demand is always optimal.

Mr. Prescott was asleep at his new home in Tempe, Ariz., when the call about the award came from Sweden.

"An important person on the Nobel committee gave me the news at 4 a.m.," Mr. Prescott said. He had just returned from a family wedding in San Francisco. His wife had stayed behind and he called her there before dawn. He also tried to reach Mr. Kydland at the university in Santa Barbara.

Mr. Prescott said he left a message on an answering machine, not knowing that Mr. Kydland was in Norway giving a guest lecture at his alma mater. In the middle of the lecture, Mr. Kydland was told there was a call from Stockholm and he broke off to take it, Reuters reported.

Mr. Kydland and Mr. Prescott began their collaboration at Carnegie Mellon while Mr. Kydland was studying for his Ph.D. and Mr. Prescott was his thesis adviser. "There were not many graduate students at Carnegie Mellon and they were like colleagues," Mr. Prescott said.

The first paper cited in the Nobel award, titled "Rules Rather than Discretion: The Inconsistency of Optimal Plans," is considered by many economists to be a valid and innovative framework for considering public policy over a wide range—not only Fed interest rate policy but policies on such matters as building homes on flood plains.

If houses go up in such high-risk areas and a flood destroys them, policy makers are faced with the question of whether to provide aid to help the victims rebuild or to let them bear the financial burden of rebuilding. Prescott-Kydland would say it is best not to provide aid, because in the long run it is better if homes are not constructed on flood plains where there is a risk of their being destroyed. While the government typically extends aid, of course, the Prescott-Kydland perspective is a useful tool for examining such policy issues, says Alan Blinder, a Princeton University economist.

"One of the hallmarks of a great intellectual achievement is that it brings into a common framework a wide variety of seemingly different problems," Mr. Blinder said.

Fiscal Growth In Latin Lands Fails to Fill Social Needs

By JUAN FORERO—April 25, 2005

QUITO, Ecuador, April 24—Last year, Ecuador's economy grew at an astounding 6.6 percent, its inflation rate was the lowest in 30 years, and foreign investment surged. Wall Street celebrated, with a New York-based analyst of Latin American economies, LatinSource, praising Ecuador for "outperforming even the most optimistic scenarios."

But those rosy numbers did not translate into better lives for Ecuador's poor or political support for Lucio Gutiérrez, who took power 28 months ago, was removed from power by Ecuador's Congress on Wednesday and who left Sunday for asylum in Brazil.

Though his interference with the judiciary was ostensibly the reason for his fall, many Ecuadoreans had become deeply disillusioned with his government, saying little had changed despite promises of more jobs, better schools and health care.

At the shabby, 57-year-old Baca Ortiz public hospital in Quito, considered the country's leading children's hospital, patients have to bring their own medicine, and doctors say they lack clean facilities, decent living wages and even the most rudimentary equipment.

"The last thing the state cares about is education and health care," said José Acosta, a staff doctor. "If the state doesn't provide medicine, doesn't provide funding, how are we supposed to provide good care?"

The discontent over a lack of state attention to basic social needs, despite increasingly positive macro-economic figures, is being played out across Latin America.

Economic growth for the region hit 5.5 percent last year, the best in a generation, inflation is down, foreign reserves are growing, and credit ratings are solid. But the positive economic news has not translated into housing for the poor, more teachers, better hospitals or social peace.

After years of fiscal prudence, privatizations and other market reforms prescribed by Washington, unemployment and poverty rates have hardly budged. Poverty, while dipping slightly last year, remains pervasive, engulfing 44 percent of the population.

"The growth rate is not always an accurate benchmark for a country's authentic prosperity," said Larry Birns, director of the Washington-based Council on Hemispheric Affairs, which tracks social and economic trends in Latin America. "Expectations have risen, and they've risen faster than the growth rate."

The high price of oil and other commodities provided by these countries is fueling the solid economic growth across Latin America. Wall Street is particularly bullish about Peru, which has had strong long-term growth. The economy of Bolivia, one of the region's poorest countries, grew by nearly 4 percent last year, while Mexico topped 4 percent and Brazil, Latin America's largest economy, registered 5.2 percent growth.

But Peru's president, Alejandro Toledo, remains the least popular leader in Latin America, and President Carlos Mesa in Bolivia has been battered by public protests. Vicente Fox's administration in Mexico is lacking popular support for its initiatives, and in Brazil many among the legions of poor believe they have been abandoned by President Luiz Inácio Lula da Silva, who embraced policies of fiscal restraint despite his leftist credentials.

The reasons for the lack of improvements are myriad, from corruption to ineptitude to poorly organized social systems. But many experts also say fiscal restraints, coupled with large public debts, are a chokehold on governments like Mr. Gutiérrez's. The public debt in many countries tops 40 percent of economic output.

"The foreign debt continues to be a factor because, far from falling, it continues to rise, and the creditors are implacable," said Augusto Ramírez Ocampo, a former foreign minister of Colombia who now works with the United Nations Development Program. "If the governments don't pay, they lose subsidies and they lose financing."

The cynicism among Latin Americans who feel shortchanged is palpable. Mónica Patiño, 44, and other parents at the 23 of May Elementary School in the poor southern part of Quito pool money to pay for blackboards, classroom benches, paint jobs and even the salaries of English and computer science teachers. Her son, Armando Estrella, 6, "is beaten by a mile compared to a private school boy," she said, noting that the poorly paid teachers deal with 45 children in a classroom.

"It's totally a mess," she said. "The education was supposed to be free. In the past, the government used to reimburse us, at least. Now they do not spend anything."

An exception is Venezuela, where a boom in oil has generated the region's highest growth—18 percent last year—providing billions of dollars that President Hugo Chávez has used to solidify his popularity by directing it into social programs.

The new government here, well aware of how Mr. Gutiérrez was debilitated, is moving in another direction. The new president, Alfredo Palacio, 66, a cardiologist and former health minister, was Mr. Gutiérrez's vice president but had long ago broken with the president over the government's fiscal restraints.

Indeed, Mr. Gutiérrez, who shifted from a critic of market reforms to a buttoned-down capitalist after he took office, had pledged to maintain fiscal discipline at all costs. He went so far as to cut subsidies for cooking fuel and food, enraging the poor.

Mr. Palacio now offers a wholesale change.

"The country needs to invest in health, education, invest in the social," he told the Quito newspaper El País. "The 6.6 percent growth that is hyped is a farce."

At Baca Ortiz, the director, Dr. Edgar Jativa, said he would like to increase salaries for doctors, who earn as little as $450 a month, and replace obsolete equipment. But he is not banking on the money arriving. "The good news will come when we get the budget," he said. "Until then, it is all just good intentions. Our presidents always have good intentions."

For Wolfowitz, Poverty Is the Newest War to Fight

By EDMUND L. ANDREWS—September 24, 2005

WASHINGTON, Sept. 23— Three months into his new job as president of the World Bank, Paul D. Wolfowitz caused heartburn this week for some former colleagues in the Bush administration.

As finance ministers from around the world began three days of discussions here on Friday, officials closed in on an international agreement to wipe out $18 billion in debt for some of the world's poorest countries. [Page C6.]

But that agreement came only after Mr. Wolfowitz publicly sided this week with officials from other countries who warned that the United States might back away from the full cost of debt relief for the poorest countries.

The quiet power struggle is part of Mr. Wolfowitz's transformation from an architect of the United States' war in Iraq to a champion for the world's poor.

Mr. Wolfowitz repeatedly called this week for "stronger commitments" by rich countries to reimburse the World Bank for lost loan repayments. He also pointedly suggested that Congress demonstrate American commitment by passing an authorization bill to cover the future costs.

"It's not that they aren't sincere," he told a group of reporters. "But time passes, and I think it's very important to keep them accountable."

American officials said that the United States made good on its promises. Hoping to mollify countries like the Netherlands, which was quietly backed by Mr. Wolfowitz, the United States produced a joint letter promising to reimburse the World Bank dollar-for-dollar on all lost repayments.

Since taking over at the World Bank, Mr. Wolfowitz has called on rich countries to provide more foreign aid. He has cultivated ties with antipoverty groups like Oxfam International and Data, the advocacy group founded by Bono, the rock star.

He has placed a new priority on Africa, but he also talks about goals like expanding opportunities for women, fighting corruption and improving governance in poor countries.

"It's not just about inputs of capital and labor," he said. "It's about a whole range of factors, and many are not traditional economic ones."

Not surprisingly, Mr. Wolfowitz has gone out of his way to reassure political leaders and antipoverty advocates who expressed concern that he would turn the World Bank into a tool of American ideology.

Some longtime campaigners against global poverty, often sharp critics of American policy, say their first impression has been good.

"It appears that he is committed to health and education, which are nearly all of the millennium development goals," said Max Lawson, policy adviser to Oxfam International, referring to goals on poverty reduction and education spelled out by members of the United Nations. "We'll be watching him very closely over the next few months to see whether he follows up on that."

But some experts said they were worried that Mr. Wolfowitz might prove too ambitious. If there is a link between his role in the Iraq war and his role at the World Bank, they caution, it may be in his fervent belief in the ability to impose democracy on countries from the outside.

"The idea that you can spread democracy by either military intervention or through the World Bank is folly, pure folly," said William Easterly, a former director of research at the World Bank and a critic of the bank's policy failures.

"What I'm afraid of is that the World Bank will have more of what it already suffers from, which is mission creep—getting involved in sweeping international causes that sound good without any evidence to show they can be accomplished."

Mr. Wolfowitz has not forgotten about Iraq. Earlier this week, he confirmed a report in The Washington Post that he was considering sending World Bank staff members into Baghdad for the first time in two years. The bank has pledged about $500 million in aid to Iraq, but withdrew its people after insurgents blew up the United Nation's mission there and killed its top envoy.

Still, Mr. Wolfowitz, the former deputy secretary of defense, has focused most of his attention elsewhere. He traveled to Africa in the summer, shortly after taking over the bank, and declared that it would be a "special emphasis" for the bank.

Moving cautiously, he has often sounded the same themes as his predecessor, James D. Wolfensohn. Like Mr. Wolfensohn, Mr. Wolfowitz talks about the importance of reducing corruption in poor countries and promoting opportunities for women.

But he has also hinted at a heavier emphasis on new agriculture technology, promoting the idea of a "green revolution" for Africa. And he has hinted at a renewed emphasis on infrastructure like roads, water systems and power plants.

Infrastructure projects are a sensitive issue for the World Bank, which retreated from them after being criticized for financing giant bridges and dams that critics said did little to relieve poverty and damaged the environment.

"We've learned a lot from our past mistakes," Mr. Wolfowitz acknowledged this week. But, he said, entrepreneurs and farmers could not begin to realize their potential if they lacked electricity, clean water or roads to move their products to market.

The World Bank makes $18 billion to $20 billion in loans and grants a year to low-income countries. But its finances depend on loan repayments and fresh donations from wealthy nations. For all its size, its scale is small in comparison with the private invest-ment that flows through Latin America and Asia.

"I don't hear any new vision yet," said Nancy Birdsall, founder of the Center on Global Development, a nonpartisan research organization here. "The big issues are not about internal management but about what the role of the World Bank is going to be in the 21st century. Right now, the banks products are still 1960's-style products—loans to governments, infrastructure loans."

Few people would argue that Mr. Wolfowitz, a former dean of Johns Hopkins School of Advanced International Studies, is short on ideas.

But supporters of increased aid to poor countries, including those who adamantly opposed Mr. Wolfowitz's role in invading Iraq, said this week that his vision for the future might be less important right now than his close relationship to President Bush.

South America Seeks to Fill the World's Table

By LARRY ROHTER—December 12, 2004

LUCAS DO RIO VERDE, Brazil—Almost overnight, South America has driven a historic global shift in food production that is turning the largely untapped frontier heartland of the continent into the world's new breadbasket.

One of the last places on earth where large tracts are still available for agriculture, the region, led by Brazil, has had an explosion of farm exports over the past decade. The growth has been fueled by a combination of market-friendly economic policies and advances in agronomy that have brought formerly unusable tropical lands into production and increased productivity levels beyond those in the United States and Europe, challenging their traditional dominance of the global farm trade.

Sometime over the next decade or so, Brazil, which Secretary of State Colin L. Powell described as "an agricultural superpower" during a visit in October, hopes to pass the United States as the world's largest agricultural producer. But the trend is far broader and can be felt also in parts of Argentina, Bolivia, Paraguay and Uruguay, with a deep impact on the region's economy and environment. And it has spurred a debate that has mainly focused on expansion into areas where the Amazon rainforest is thought to be jeopardized.

"There has been a silent revolution in the countryside" since the 1990's, Brazil's minister of agriculture, Roberto Rodrigues, said in an interview in the capital, Brasília. The past four or five years in particular, he said, have been "characterized by spectacular growth and a huge increase in demand" abroad for foodstuffs, which has given Brazil "the capacity to compete with anyone."

The global effect has been powerful. In June, the United States imported more in farm products than it sold abroad, further evidence of its eroding position. Alert to the challenge, the Iowa Farm Bureau Federation even has a presentation for its members called "Should Brazil Give You Heartburn?" The answer is a not-so-qualified yes.

The competition is personified in producers like Otaviano Pivetta, 45, and Helmute Lawisch, 39. Less than 20 years ago, the two friends took turns driving 1,500 miles over mostly bone-jarring roads from their homes in Brazil's southern-most state to stake their claim in this region, which was mostly jungle then, with little in the way of electricity, sanitation or other public services.

In retrospect, it is clear that they were in the vanguard of a fundamental transformation of global agriculture. Today, farmland stretches to the horizon. With a climate that varies little the year round, it is not unusual to have two or even three harvests a year and to see combines clearing fields with planters sowing another crop in their wake.

The two men are now among the most successful producers in the region, and Mr. Pivetta has twice been elected mayor of Lucas do Rio Verde. Each now cultivates more than 100,000 acres, sending soybeans, cotton and pork to markets as distant as China, Russia and Pakistan. With the Southern Hemisphere's spring planting season now complete, the two farmers and scores of others like them here in Mato Grosso state are looking forward to another year of bumper crops.

"With the great climate and fertile soil we have here, I can't imagine any other place that gets the kind of productivity that we do," said Mr. Pivetta, whose family now runs a half-dozen farms here. "Not in Brazil or anywhere else are you going to find two crops a year yielding three tons of grain an acre."

Brazil's 'Green Anchor'

Agriculture is now a $150-billion-a-year business in Brazil, accounting for more than 40 percent of the country's exports and creating what Brazilians call the "green anchor" of their economy.

Already the world's biggest exporter of chickens, orange juice, sugar, coffee and tobacco, according to Agriculture Ministry statistics, Brazil soon hopes to add soybeans to the list, depending on what happens in that volatile market.

With a grass-fed herd of 175 million cattle that is the world's largest, it passed the United States as the world's largest exporter of beef last year. During the first nine months of 2004, sales of Brazilian beef abroad rose 77 percent over the same period last year, leading the government to predict $2.5 billion in earnings from beef exports this year.

Over all, the agricultural bonanza, aided in part by mad cow disease in Europe and avian flu in Asia, is likely to give Brazil a record trade surplus of over $30 billion.

Brazil's advantages start with the availability of large amounts of cheap land, especially here in this region of well-drained tropical savanna known as the cerrado. Larger than the American grain belt but dismissed as useless for farming until barely a quarter of a century ago, the cerrado cuts across the heart of Brazil, and its vastness permits economies of scale that are the envy of producers elsewhere.

"What's really driving this revolution is that the Brazilians discovered how to use tropical and savanna soils that had always been considered poor," said G. Edward Schuh, director of the Center for International Economic Policy at the University of Minnesota. "They learned that with modest applications of lime and phosphorus they can quadruple and quintuple their yields, not just with soybeans but also with maize, cotton and other commodities."

The discovery of how to enrich the soil and make it highly productive came in research at the Brazilian Enterprise for Agricultural and Livestock Research, a government agency known by the Portuguese-language acronym Embrapa. The agency's biggest successes, however, have been in modifying crops to grow in those altered soils.

Until recently, for example, soybeans were not thought to flourish in tropical soils and climates. But researchers at Embrapa and similar private or state institutes have developed more than 40 varieties of soy specially adapted for the cerrado. Soybeans now account for nearly half of Brazil's farm exports and are the main crop in this region.

Embrapa researchers have also developed breeds of cattle for the tropics, using a variety originally from India, as well as a "tropical hog" that is lower in fat and cholesterol than its American counterpart and that has a higher ham and loin yield. Perhaps most surprisingly, the Brazilians are also working on varieties of tropical wheat.

"One of the main reasons we believe that Brazil has a greater chance to prosper even further is that they have a very solid scientific foundation," said Daniel Lederman, an economist at the World Bank who specializes in agriculture. "The concept of tropical technology is very attractive and we are learning a lot by studying Embrapa, which is at the forefront of applied agricultural research."

Government's Helping Hand

Changes in economic policies have also spurred the boom here. At the beginning of the 1990's, for example, Brazil lifted longtime restrictions on imports, leading to a surge in purchases of tractors, combines, fertilizers, pesticides and seeds.

A leap in exports came in 1999, when the government devalued the currency and allowed the real, which had been trading at near par with the dollar, to float on the currency exchange market. Today, the real trades at almost three to the dollar, which means incomes for agricultural producers have nearly tripled.

The Brazilian bonanza has been eagerly welcomed by the main international agricultural trading companies, which have been quick to seize new opportunities. In this town of 30,000, Archer Daniels Midland, Bunge and Cargill not only have built huge warehouses and silos along the main highway, but have also provided credit to farmers on a scale far beyond the means of the Brazilian government.

"It's good business for them, but we have to admit we owe a lot to the trading companies," said Mr. Lawisch, whose family, modest stakeholders in their home state of Rio Grande do Sul, has moved here. "When we needed them, they supported us, and now that we are prospering, our commercial relationship continues to expand every year."

To counter the South American advances, the United States and Europe have increased subsidies to their own beleaguered farmers. But in a pair of landmark decisions, the World Trade Organization recently ruled that such subsidies for cotton and sugar are illegal and must be phased out.

The Bush administration is appealing the cotton ruling, but it is widely expected to lose, and many economists say the principle could be applied to other crops.

All of this clearly will have an increasing impact on agriculture in the United States. Experts say some areas that are not competitive with South America may have to move from one crop to another, while others will face pressure to shift out of agriculture altogether.

Some American and European farmers already have, and are starting to buy farmland here. Wolfgang Hudepohl, a real estate agent in Cuiabá, Mato Grosso's state capital, estimates that he has sold 60 farms to foreigners over the past few years. "Foreigners like not only the cheap prices, but also the low production costs and the fact they are not tied down by regulations," he said.

At the edges of the agricultural frontier, in states like Maranhão and Piauí hundreds of miles east of here, land is still remarkably cheap, as little as $20 an acre in some remote areas. But in places where the boom is already going full blast, like here, land prices are rising rapidly.

"Seven years ago, I bought 6,175 acres, and paid $125,000," said Jose Luiz Lorenzi, a farmer and manager of the John Deere agency here, which is the busiest in Brazil. "Just recently I got an offer of $1.5 million for the same land. But I'm not selling. I want to buy more property myself because there is no better investment in the world than buying land in Mato Grosso."

The Costs of the Boom

The real estate boom has not been without social tensions and other costs, particularly to the environment, as the expansion of farm and grazing lands has accelerated Amazon deforestation. Typically, jungle is razed for conversion first into cattle pasture and then, as the agricultural frontier advances, into fields for soybeans and other crops.

But producers in the cerrado, which is more than 1,000 miles from the coast, say they are more concerned about the lack of reliable highways, railways and barge routes, which adds to the cost of doing business. That situation, farmers say, is gradually improving, as is Brazil's ability to weather the ups and downs of agricultural markets.

After nearly a decade of rising prices and record profits, soybean prices, for instance, have sharply dropped this year, the result in large part of a decision to curb imports and to cancel existing contracts by China, where a huge new market has emerged to satisfy the changing diet of a growing middle class.

In the past, when Brazilian agriculture was dependent on a single crop, that would have spelled certain disaster. But Brazil has made a successful effort to diversify its exports, and has reduced its vulnerability to sudden price fluctuations for any single crop. In the 1960's, for example, coffee was responsible for 60 percent of Brazil's exports. Today, coffee is seventh on the list.

As a result, the watchword today for Brazilian farm producers is to diversify even further.

"We're entering a phase in which we're not going just to be growing things, but processing them too, turning them into finished products," said Eledir Pedro Techio, manager of the local credit cooperative and a soybean and corn farmer. It is also clear that further gains in production are still to come, thanks both to expansion of the agricultural frontier and higher yields.

Government officials estimate that an additional 50 million acres, much of it as potentially fertile as the land being tilled here now, are likely to be put into production over the next decade.

"There's no way you can go wrong here," Mr. Lawisch said. "We're champions of production already, but we think we can do even better. We aim to feed not just Brazil, but the world."

What Happened When Two Countries Liberalized Trade? Pain, Then Gain

By VIRGINIA POSTREL—January 27, 2005

ECONOMISTS argue for free trade. They have two centuries of theory and experience to back them up. And they have recent empirical studies of how the liberalization of trade has increased productivity in less-developed countries like Chile and India. Lowering trade barriers, they maintain, not only cuts costs for consumers but aids economic growth and makes the general public better off.

Even so, free trade is a tough sell. "The truth of the matter is that we have one heck of a time explaining these benefits to the larger public, a public gripped by free trade fatigue," the economist Daniel Trefler wrote in an article last fall in The American Economic Review.

One problem, he argued, is that there is not enough research on how free trade affects industrialized countries like the United States and Canada. Another is that research tends to concentrate on either long-term benefits or on short-term costs, instead of looking at both.

"We talk a lot about the benefits of free trade agreements, but when it comes to academics studying it, we know next to nothing in terms of hard-core facts about what happens when two rich countries liberalize trade," Professor Trefler, of the Rotman School of Management at the University of Toronto, said in an interview.

His article, "The Long and Short of the Canada-U.S. Free Trade Agreement," uses detailed data on both Canadian industries and individual companies to address these gaps. (The paper is on his Web site at http://www.economics.utoronto.ca/trefler/) The study looks at the effect of tariff reductions, the simplest kind of liberalization.

Tariffs are usually not considered that significant in developed countries, where many major industries compete without such protection. But, Professor Trefler said, "they're not significant except where they matter."

Before the agreement went into effect in 1989, more than one in four Canadian industries were, in fact, protected by tariffs of more than 10 percent. Those industries included not only businesses known for their protectionism, notably apparel makers, but manufacturers of a wide range of products, from beer and pretzels to coffins, plastic pipes and paper bags.

Before the agreement, imports from the United States faced an average tariff of 8.1 percent and an effective tariff of 16 percent. The effective rate included import taxes on the final product and tariffs paid on raw materials. Someone importing a chair could face a direct tariff on furniture, for example, but could also pay indirect tariffs on wood and upholstery fabric.

Not surprisingly, the Canadian industries that had relied on tariffs to protect them "were hammered" when those barriers disappeared, Professor Trefler said. "They saw their employment fall by 12 percent," he said, meaning one in eight workers lost their jobs. In manufacturing as a whole, the trade agreement reduced employment by 5 percent.

"Employment losses of 5 percent translate into 100,000 lost jobs and strike me as large," he wrote, "not least because only a relatively small number of industries experienced deep tariff concessions."

No wonder free trade agreements touch off so much opposition.

As painful as those layoffs were, however, the job losses were a short-term effect. Over the long run, employment in Canada did not drop, and manufacturing employment remains more robust than in other industrialized countries.

"Within 10 years, the lost employment was made up by employment gains in other parts of manufacturing," Professor Trefler found.

While low-productivity plants shut down, high-productivity Canadian manufacturers not only expanded into the United States but further improved their operations. Along the way, they hired enough new workers to make up for losses elsewhere.

"The average effect of the U.S. tariff cuts on Canadian employment was thus a wash: the employment losses by less-productive firms offset the employment gains by more productive firms," Professor Trefler wrote in an e-mail message, citing further research.

Nor, contrary to predictions, did Canadian wages drop because of competition from less-educated, nonunionized workers in the southern United States. Quite the opposite: using payroll statistics, he found that "for all workers, the tariff concessions raised annual earnings" by about 3 percent over eight years.

Admittedly, that is not a lot. "A 3 percent rise in earnings spread over eight years will buy you more than a cup of coffee, but not at Starbucks," he wrote. "The important finding is not that earnings went up, but that earnings did not go down." In addition, he said, "there is absolutely no evidence" that the trade agreement worsened income inequality.

The big story is that lowering tariffs set off a productivity boom.

Formerly sheltered Canadian companies began to compete with and compare themselves with more-efficient American businesses. Some went under, but others significantly improved operations.

The productivity gains were huge. In the formerly sheltered industries most affected by the tariff cuts, labor productivity jumped 15 percent, at least half from closing inefficient plants. "This translates into an enormous compound annual growth rate of 1.9 percent," he wrote.

But closing plants is not the whole story, or even half of it. Among export-oriented industries, which expanded after the agreement, data from individual plants show an increase in labor productivity of 14 percent. Manufacturing productivity as a whole jumped 6 percent.

"The idea that a simple government policy could raise productivity so dramatically is to me truly remarkable," Professor Trefler said.

And the long-run increase in productivity did not result mostly from shutting down inefficient plants. It came from better operating practices.

"That's not coming from natural selection," he said. "That firm's actually doing business differently."

Thanks in part to the trade agreement, he sees a shift in attitudes among the younger generation of Canadian managers. They are less content to be the best in Canada's relatively small market.

"They're thinking the competition isn't here in Toronto," he said. "The competition is there in the U.S. To succeed in U.S. markets, you have to play like the Americans do, which is innovate and upgrade."

Virginia Postrel (http://www.dynamist.com) is the author of "The Substance of Style: How the Rise of Aesthetic Value Is Remaking Commerce, Culture and Consciousness," just published in paperback by Perennial.

Moody's Raises a Key Debt Rating on Brazil

By TODD BENSON—September 10, 2004

SÃO PAULO, Brazil, Sept. 9— Moody's Investors Service, the credit rating agency, upgraded Brazil's sovereign debt rating on Thursday, saying strong exports and prudent debt management had helped make the country, South America's largest economy, less vulnerable to sudden swings in market sentiment.

In what many analysts said was a long overdue move, Moody's raised Brazil's long-term foreign currency rating to B1 from B2, putting it four notches below investment grade and on par with other heavily indebted emerging market countries like Turkey. The upgrade also put Moody's rating on Brazil in line with those of other credit agencies including Standard & Poor's and Fitch Ratings.

"It's no surprise, but it's still very good news," said Mário Mesquita, chief economist at ABN Amro in São Paulo. "What Moody's is basically saying is that the growth in exports is making it easier for Brazil to service its debt."

The upgrade may help reduce borrowing costs for Brazil, which is saddled with a public-sector debt burden equal to 55 percent of gross domestic product. But already the rates it has to pay on its debt are receding. Brazil sold 750 million euros of eight-year bonds on Wednesday at a price to yield 8.7 percent, down from the 11.5 percent yield it paid to sell seven-year bonds in 2002.

Record exports of products like soybeans, steel and cars are also reducing Brazil's dependency on foreign borrowing by bringing in much-needed dollars. Exports have surged more than 33 percent so far this year to $62.7 billion, putting the country on track to rack up a record $90 billion in exports in 2004, according to the trade ministry. Because of the strong exports, Brazil is expected to post a trade surplus this year of about $30 billion, up from a record surplus of $24.8 billion in 2003.

Moody's also said that the Brazilian government's efforts to reduce the volatility of its debt burden were bearing fruit, helping to shield the country from swings in market sentiment or a sharp devaluation of its currency, the real.

"The authorities have also substantially improved the composition of the domestic bond debt by increasing the share of fixed interest-rate debt and reducing the share of dollar-linked debt," Moody's said.

Since President Luiz Inácio Lula da Silva took office in January 2003, the central bank has reduced the ratio of the government's domestic debt linked to the dollar from 37 percent to about 14 percent—its lowest level ever—by aggressively buying back maturing securities indexed to the dollar.

Brazil's sovereign debt spreads, or the premium the country must pay over comparable United States Treasury bonds to borrow money abroad, narrowed 10 basis points to 495 basis points shortly after Moody's announced the upgrade, according to the J. P. Morgan Emerging Markets Bond Index Plus. Tighter spreads indicate improving investor confidence in Brazil.

China Revalues the Yuan

July 22, 2005

CHINA'S currency revaluation was not as big as the blame-Beijing-first crowd in Congress has been demanding. But it is the start of something big, and now it's up to Congress to show equal sense.

For more than a decade, China has fixed the exchange rate of its currency, the yuan, to the dollar. That provided stability, helping China to weather the Asian financial crisis in 1997 and 1998 and supporting its subsequent economic growth. But in recent months, some members of Congress have threatened China with punitive tariffs, claiming that the practice of fixing the yuan to the dollar made Chinese products artificially cheap on global markets and hurt American exports. They overstated their case, but the political threat was clear.

To its credit, the administration has tried to restrain the Congressional neoprotectionists. That bought the Chinese some time, and yesterday, they acted. They loosely linked the yuan's value to a basket of currencies, pushing it up 2 percent against the dollar immediately and leaving open the possibility of a larger appreciation in the weeks and months ahead.

The China bashers have been hoping for a revaluation of 10 percent or more, and we'll know better in the near future how far China is prepared to go. Right now, it is important to applaud China's willingness to act, and acknowledge the very substantial risks it is taking. The revaluation, for instance, is likely to attract currency speculators who will pour in the kind of money that feeds bubbles, which can burst with disastrous consequences.

The anti-China crowd in Congress should also get serious about making a lasting dent in the budget deficit. Doing so would address global imbalances more effectively than a yuan revaluation because it would reduce the nation's need to borrow billions of dollars a day from abroad. In fact, the sooner Congress can see international imbalances as a problem largely of America's own making, the better.

When China was rigidly fixing its exchange rate, it did so by buying vast amounts of United States Treasuries. Under its new flexible currency regime, the day may come when China will not need to buy as many Treasuries. But unless Washington curbs its deficits, the United States could still need China to buy its securities, and that situation could lead to sharply higher United States interest rates.

China needs a more flexible currency mainly to manage its own economy better. But the move should also be good for international trade relations if the United States can rise to the occasion.